WHAT SHAT THAT

THE POCKET GUIDE TO POOP IDENTITY

MATT
PAGETT

TEN SPEED PRESS
Berkeley | Toronto

Copyright © 2007 by Quid Publishing

Ten Speed Press
PO Box 7123
Berkeley, California 94707
www.tenspeed.com

Distributed in Canada by Ten Speed Press Canada.

Conceived, designed, and produced by
Quid Publishing
Level 4 Sheridan House
114 Western Road
Hove BN3 1DD
United Kingdom
www.quidpublishing.com

Cover design by Ed Anderson

Library of Congress Cataloging-in-Publication Data
is on file with the publisher.

ISBN-13: 978-1-58008-885-5
ISBN-10: 1-58008-885-6

Printed in China
First printing, 2007

1 2 3 4 5 6 7 8 9 10 — 11 10 09 08 07

NOTE
The author, publisher, and copyright holder assume no responsibility for any injury, loss, or damage caused or sustained as a consequence of the use and application of the contents of this book.

Contents

591.5

P 147

Introduction

The dung of other animals is not quite as discomforting for us to discuss as our own. In fact, it is packed with nuggets of interest. As this book shows, animal dung is rich in information and uses, for humans, plants, and the animals themselves. Humans have for centuries used it as fuel, insulation, and fertilizer, for sport and entertainment. Plants are able to germinate and spread because of it. And for animals, dung is lived in, bred in, and fed on. It also helps protect them from disease and predation.

A NOTE ON STRUCTURE

Taxonomy is the science of organism classification, and this book has been organized around that system. Each animal is listed alphabetically according to its taxonomical family name, starting with the eagle (*Accipitridae*) and ending with the wombat (*Vombatidae*).

While humans may have evolved out of the caves and given up hunting and gathering in favor of skinny lattes at the mall, one thing remains as an inescapable part of being an animal—and that is the act of defecation. Just as the need to breathe and the need for food unite all, so does the need to poop.

The animal body is like a machine, with highly complex processes involving chemicals and gases, actions and reactions. The poop payoff—brown, dirty, and smelly though it is—is inevitable. It is like steam rising from a factory chimney or fumes pumped from a car tailpipe, except in this case a wholly natural emission.

Not that animal dung is without its uses. It is critical in terms of conservation, for example, and is playing a leading role in the survival of several species. Methods of scientific analysis are constantly improving, and now much can be revealed about the depositor—its age, sex, size, diet, habitat, relationship with other animals, and so on—helping scientists gain a greater understanding of how the animal lives.

Dung's make-up can also be exploited for the greater good of the environment. Thus, cow dung can be used to make greener gases, llama dung for cleaning contaminated water, and plankton poop has the ability to store carbon.

Not everything about dung smells so sweet, however. It contains toxins, germs, and bacteria that can kill. It can corrode metal and stain your carpet. It can damage plant life and upset ecosystems. And it stinks—sometimes a lot. Nature is not a gentle, benign, Disney-style backdrop to our much more important lives. It is dynamic, ever-changing, fascinating, and at times brutal and messy. And the dung the animals provide is a true reflection of this.

As well as having many features specific to different animals, poop raises some interesting general questions. A few of the most obvious ones are tackled on the next page.

▼ Moose poop is hard to avoid in Alaskan souvenir shops (see pages 32–33).

▲ **Chimpanzee poo has been implicated in the spread of HIV (see pages 54–55).**

RECYCLING THE RECYCLED

Zoo dung presents something of a disposal problem. The residents of Toronto Zoo, for example, produce 5.75 tons (5,219 kg) of it every day. Multiply that by the 10,000 zoos worldwide, and that's some pile to get rid of. Some recycle it as biofuel or compost.

What is poop made from?

Different animals make different dung, and even the same animal can make different dung, depending on diet and health. Generally, though, the wetter the poop, the larger the amount of unused water the body is expelling. Other components include dead bacteria that have helped digest the food, fiber that has helped it move through the gut, live bacteria, proteins, dead cells, intestinal mucus, microbes, and fats.

The other most noticeable element is undigested food. Carnivore dung can bear traces of hair, fur, feathers, and bone, which all help to bind the stool together. Meat is protein-rich and easy to digest, meaning carnivores don't need to go that often. The limited diet of herbivores, on the other hand, is harder to digest, so they have to eat more—and poop a whole heap more as well. Remnants of vegetation will often be visible, and because as much water is absorbed by the body as possible, their dung is drier.

Why does poop smell?

Dung contains bacteria, some of which produce organic compounds like skatole and indole, and these contain high amounts of noxious gases like nitrogen and sulfur. What an animal eats will also affect how bad the smell is. The high-fiber diet of most herbivores, for example, produces far less nixous poop than a carnivore's high protein intake.

Why is poop brown?

As the liver breaks down hemoglobin in red blood cells, so it produces the pigment bilirubin. This finds its way to the intestine, gets worked on by more bacteria, and colors the dung.

Animal poo isn't always brown, however, and bird poo is, of course, white. Why? The white component is actually a form of urine called uric acid. The kidneys extract nitrogenous waste from the bloodstream, which is dunged with the poop from the animal's cloaca, a common vent for both waste products.

▼ Rooting around: some animals think nothing of redigesting their own dung (see pages 76–77).

Eagle

Class: Aves
Order: Falconiformes
Family: Accipitridae
Genera: Various; species include Bald (*Haliaeetus leucocephalus*) and Golden (*Aquila chrysaetos*)
Distribution: Worldwide
Habitat: Various, including mountains and open plains
Diet: Omnivorous

An incredibly powerful bird of prey, the eagle has come to represent and symbolize everything from a Portuguese soccer team to God himself. Its grace, expertise, and strength, combined with its often being found in remote areas, all contribute to its almost mystical reputation. Seeing one defecate is rather like imagining royalty on the toilet: the mystery is punctured, and we are reminded that they are just like us after all.

MESS FACTOR

4 out of 5

Description

The eagle's stomach is well equipped to deal with its varied diet. Strong digestive acids help absorb the food, and feathers, fur, and bone fragments are regurgitated as pellets rather than passed out in the feces. The color of droppings varies, depending on diet. As with all other birds and some animals, the eagle dungs through a cloaca, and uric acid is passed out with the fecal matter, as opposed to peeing and pooping separately.

Acid Drop(ping)s

The eagle's droppings are normally highly acidic, due to the strength of its digestive juices, as mentioned above. A streak of eagle poop has the power to corrode, so it is always advisable to remove it as quickly as possible from vulnerable areas. In 1998, bald eagles on Kodiak Island, Alaska, caused headaches for a local power supplier. Accumulations of their acidic poop started to eat into metallic elements on the electricity poles they had been using as perches, electrocuting the birds and causing expensive power outages. So, the forward-thinking power company created a device that safely diverted the eagles away from the poles, and has since won awards for its work in the field of dung deterrence.

In wilder areas such as the Arctic, eagle dung is helping scientists identify and monitor the birds' territories. As they continually perch on the same rocks, watching out for prey or predators, the slow build-up of droppings provides enough nutrition for the jewel lichens (*Xanthoria elegans*) to take root. Bright orange in color, these hardy plants have the advantage of being easily spotted from the air, allowing researchers in planes or helicopters to hone in on specific areas without having to trudge through sometimes inhospitable terrain. A kind of flame-colored, poo-fertilized "come-and-get-me," if you like.

LOVE BIRD

Presenting an old Chinese aphrodisiac recipe. Take some eagle droppings; add the semen of a young man; mix together and consume. Feeling horny yet?

◀ **Streaks of highly acidic eagle poop are fine on rocks, but can damage more vulnerable surfaces.**

Cow

Order: Artiodactyla

Family: Bovidae

Genus: Bos (species *B. taurus*)

Distribution: Worldwide, except Antarctica

Habitat: Various, but always in need of adequate grazing area

Diet: Herbivorous, including grasses, stems, other plant matter

There are almost as many uses for cow dung (insulation, heating, soil fertilization, sport) as there are uses for the animal itself (meat, milk and dairy products, leather). Not bad for a substance whose name is used to denote something worthless. So, in many ways, bullshit is not bullshit at all.

MESS FACTOR

4 out of 5

Description

There are two varieties of cow dung, depending upon what the animal has been eating. Succulent grass leads to a brown or greenish semiliquid mass, which will then dry to a large flat chip once it's been laid. Drier food, on the other hand, will result in several smaller and firmer layered chips. Its initially strong smell fades with time. An average cow lays about ten chips a day, and they are generally deposited in feeding areas or just as the cow walks along.

In Cud We Trust

All cows are ruminants, meaning they have a special system of digestion and re-digestion. Their stomachs are composed of four chambers, which allows the food they ingest to be regurgitated

▲ **Pies, pats, chips, meadow muffins, or country pancakes—call it what you like, cow poop is truly versatile.**

as cud, re-chewed, and re-swallowed. This in turn allows the animal's body to extract as many nutrients as it possibly can, which is necessary because its diet is not the richest in terms of energy, proteins, and so on. From mouth to dung is a process that can take as long as 100 hours, one of the slowest food passage rates in the entire animal kingdom.

A Piece of the Pie

Developing countries such as Nepal are increasingly using cow dung to produce biogas, an environmentally friendly alternative to fossil fuels like coal and oil. The dung is stored in airless containers where, thanks to the absence of oxygen, it is broken down by bacteria already present. The addition of water creates a chemical reaction, resulting in a gas composed of 70 percent methane, which is burnt domestically and thus prevented from entering the Earth's atmosphere. The remaining slurry ends up as compost. Cow dung thus creates employment, cleaner lives, and—through the energy trade-off scheme introduced by the Kyoto Protocol—more money for developing countries. It's good shit, man.

CHIP CHUCK

The 2006 Men's World Championship Cow Chip Throw in Beaver, Oklahoma, was won by James Pratt with a throw of 200.7 feet (61 m). The Women's Championship was won by Dana Martin who recorded a toss of 138.6 feet (42 m).

13

Gazelle

Order:	Artiodactyla
Family:	Bovidae
Genus:	*Gazella*; species include Chinkara (*G. bennettii*) and Thomson's (*G. thomsonii*)
Distribution:	Africa, Southwest and Central Asia
Habitat:	Grassland and savanna
Diet:	Herbivorous, mainly plants, grasses, leaves

Thanks to its slender body and nimble legs, the gazelle is an excellent runner, with some species able to run at up to 50 MPH. Its senses of sight and smell are also strong. It can cover large distances quite easily, and it travels in herds, which, during migration season, can number in their thousands. Gazelle dung is rich in history, though the defecatory habits of at least one species raise fears for its future.

MESS FACTOR

2 out of 5

Description

As a member of the family Bovidae (together with cows, sheep, and deer), the gazelle has a four-chambered stomach, allowing it to extract as much goodness as possible from the plants it eats. Gazelles don't need much water (indeed some never drink water at all, gaining all liquid refreshment from vegetation) and so their dung is dry and fibrous. It is deposited in feeding areas and also in common areas called middens.

Multipurpose and 100 Percent Natural

Gazelle dung was used in a variety of ways in ancient Egypt. One of the oldest medicinal documents ever discovered is the Ebers Papyrus, which dates back to around 1550 B.C.E. Featured in it is a recipe for hair tonic prepared from myrtle (a red mineral), kohl, oil, hippopotamus fat, and gazelle droppings. Physicians also used the dung against infections and inflammations, and, when dried, it was commonly used as domestic fuel. Elsewhere, fumes from gazelle dung were widely acknowledged to be an effective rodent repellant, so it was often laid in grain stores.

Drop-ln(g) Center

As social animals, some gazelle species (such as Grant's gazelle) display what's termed "selective defecation"—that is, a herd will collectively dung in a specific location. For the gazelles themselves, this could be a method of self-medication, keeping all the dung's bacteria and parasites in one known place. It could also perform a communicative role within a group (poop contains many olfactory messages). However, such an arrangement leaves them susceptible to poachers, who value the animals for their meat, horns, skins, and so on. Middens are usually situated at a prominent landmark, are visually conspicuous (as a large pile of poo is likely to be), and gazelles usually visit them at night.

SCAT FACT

Eighty percent of the Mongolian gazelle's summer diet consists of onion, so if their scat doesn't smell, their breath certainly will.

▼ A fine set of rich, dark droppings, fresh from the rear of a Dama gazelle.

Sheep

Order: Artiodactyla
Family: Bovidae
Genus: *Ovis* (species *O. aries*)
Distribution: Worldwide, except Antarctica
Habitat: Various, including farmland, moorland, mountains
Diet: Herbivorous, including grasses and lichens

As with other domesticated farm animals, the sheep has various uses, both as a source of meat, milk, and wool, and also for its ability to manage pastures by grazing. The seemingly harmless, tidy pellets it deposits have also served a similarly wide range of purposes, both at home and out in the field.

MESS FACTOR

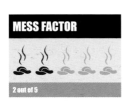

2 out of 5

Description

Sheep leave a series of small round or oval pellets made up of fine plant material. The sheep is a ruminant, absorbing as many nutrients from its food as it can. This includes water, resulting in very dry dung. Their poo has a strong, grassy odor and is found in the animals' feeding areas.

The Advantages of Poo

Because the sheep has become such a domesticated animal, it and its dung have become the focus for much research. Findings have important implications for farmers, and can lead to the development of potentially lucrative products for the research funders. One example is a device enabling farmers to test their flocks' droppings for signs of parasitic infection.

The Disadvantages of Poo

Sheep-poo analysis can reveal much about both the biology of the animal and the impact it has on its environment. Studies have shown that extensive overgrazing by sheep and other livestock has resulted in the degradation of natural ecosystems, complicated by the dropping of their dung. The high quantities of nitrogen in sheep poo, for example, together with the increase in atmospheric nitrogen (due to the burning of fossil fuels), has, in some areas, limited the range of plant life in the newly fertilized soil.

Diverse Dung

Domestically, sheep poo has been used for heating, cooking, and for firing pottery. A favorite smoked meat in Iceland is *hangikjöt*, a piece of either lamb, mutton, or horse. The meat is hung above a fire, which is made with fuel traditionally composed of dried, pressed sheep dung mixed with straw gathered from the sheep pens. The process can take up to three weeks, after which it is eaten on special occasions.

▲ **While sheep poop may look and smell pretty harmless, it does in fact have a darker, more destructive side.**

PIECES OF FECES

In a recent incident, two pieces of dung appeared in a lamb that was being carved for a Sunday lunch in Norway. "Eating a roast lamb with excrement is probably not dangerous, as it has been heat-treated," said a company spokesman.

Yak

Order: Artiodactyla
Family: Bovidae
Genus: *Bos* (species *B. grunniens*)
Distribution: Tibetan plateau
Habitat: Grassland and sparse upland
Diet: Herbivorous, including grasses, shrubs, moss

The semi-domesticated yak is to Tibet what the llama is to Bolivia: it is used for carrying goods (its wide hooves are perfectly suited to the hilly terrain), its fur is used to make clothing, blankets, and tents, and its meat and milk are consumed. Visit the Tibetan mountains and you will also see masses of flattened dung pats in various formations, drying out in the sun or all stored up waiting to be used as fuel in this virtually treeless area. It is a traditional sight that has a political resonance as Tibet progresses into the twenty-first century.

MESS FACTOR

4 out of 5

Description

As part of the same genus, it's unsurprising that yak dung is similar to that of the cow. Being a ruminant, all food is eaten, regurgitated, and re-chewed as cud before it makes it through to the rest of the yak's digestive system. The resulting dung is moist and very fibrous, still bearing traces of grass. The dung is either brown or black.

The Perfect Patty

Before it is used as a fuel source, yak dung is formed into patties measuring about 8 inches (20 cm) across. A stick covered in yak hair is used to cut the dung into 0.3 inches (1 cm) thick slices, which are then left out in the sun to dry, often stuck onto the sides of buildings. The dried patties are then stacked in heaps until needed, and may get painted with fresh poo to keep out the rain. In some localities, the patties are also used like bricks—stacked in layers to make pens in which the yak are kept during the cold season—and the moist dung can be painted onto wooden fencing to fill in cracks, much like cement.

Shock of the New

In 2006, Chinese authorities launched the world's highest railroad through yak country, linking Golmund in the Chinese northwestern province with the Tibetan capital, Lhasa, a distance of 709 miles (1,142 km). Some Tibetans hope the railroad will bring modern comforts such as electricity and coal to the area, while the Chinese government has urged the Tibetans to carry on using yak dung because of its environmental benefits. With such a gleaming symbol of progress and modernity snaking its way through an area as rooted in tradition as the Tibetan plateau, there seems potential for disquiet.

SHIT HOT, SHIT COLD

Dried yak dung burns hot and has no significant odor. It doesn't retain heat well, though, so once it burns out, the ambient temperature soon plummets again.

▶ **Yak patties drying in the sun—a common sight in Tibet, but for how much longer?**

Sloth

Order: Pilosa

Family: Bradypodidae and Megalonychidae

Genera: Two-toed (*Choloepus*) and three-toed (*Bradypus*)

Distribution: Central and South America

Habitat: Forest

Diet: Omnivorous, mainly plant material, but will also eat some insects and lizards

The life of a sloth turns much biological thinking upside down. The animal averages a speed of about 1 foot per minute, it sleeps for 16 hours a day, and it does indeed spend most of its time hanging upside down from tree branches. Its defecatory habits are similarly unique and continue to puzzle naturalists. The questions they raise only add to the mystery surrounding one of nature's most idiosyncratic creatures.

MESS FACTOR

3 out of 5

Description

Due to the large amount of plant material in their diet, sloth poo is very fibrous. Its stomach is astonishingly large (constituting about a third of its total body volume) and the digestive process can take up to a month, resulting in a very slow metabolism. Having been such a long time in the making, sloth dung is relatively hard and takes a long time to decompose.

WHY???

About once a week, the sloth leaves the forest canopy, expending much valuable energy and exposing itself to the risk of potential predation, to defecate and urinate at the tree base. A number

▲ **Having been a long time in the making, sloth dung is hard and fibrous—and very mysterious.**

SCAT FACT

In 1998, fossilized dung dating back 19,000 years was excavated in a cave near Las Vegas. It had been deposited by a giant sloth, an animal the size of an elephant. The giant sloth lived on the ground, which the trees were probably quite happy about.

of suggestions have been put forward as to why the animal does this: it would poop over itself otherwise; it is helping to fertilize the tree; the sound of its pellets falling through the foliage would reveal its presence to predators; it is an ingrained genetic behavior from when its ancestors still lived on the ground; it is providing a service to the beneficial parasites that live in its fur; or it is a form of territorial marking. Some of these hold more water than others, though it is something that maybe will never be completely understood.

Caring and Sharing

That relationship it has with its parasites is worth further elaboration. As well as a form of algae that grows on its fur, various insects like to get similarly cozy with the sloth. And just as its body is a perfect place to live, its dung is a similarly perfect place to breed. One particular moth will journey down the tree on the animal's back, crawl onto the dung, and lay its eggs in time for another lift back up. The eggs then hatch into larvae that feed on, and develop and pupate in, the dung, ready to fly off and join another sloth elsewhere.

21

Llama

Order: Artiodactyla

Family: Camelidae

Genus: *Lama* (species *L. glama*)

Distribution: Commonly found in South America, also introduced in parts of North America, Europe, and Australia

Habitat: Highlands and shrubland

Diet: Herbivorous, mainly grasses and shrubs

Seventy percent (3 million) of the total global llama population can be found in Bolivia, watched over by native herdsmen. They can also be found in Argentina, Ecuador, Chile, and Peru, as well as on farms further afield. Since the time of the Incas, llamas have been used for transportation, textiles, and even protecting sheep. Their dung has its uses, too, with one particular venture being of potentially great environmental benefit.

MESS FACTOR

3 out of 5

Description

Similar to the droppings of sheep, llama dung consists of a series of small pellets, deposited in clumps. They are usually brown and virtually odorless. The llama is a ruminant with three stomachs, enabling its body to gain extra nutrients via cud-chewing. Like gazelles, llamas defecate in communal areas known as latrines. Latrines are beneficial because they contain the risk of parasitic infection, and also serve as territorial markers.

A Crock of Shit?

One apocryphal tale has it that, sometime during the early 1940s, the U.S. army—in accordance with traditional specifications—needed a large batch of llama dung to treat the leather on its airplane seats. Only after an attempt to establish a breeding herd failed did anyone think to question the dung's dubious role in this process. After some research, it was found that the edict dated back to the British Empire, when llama dung would be rubbed into fresh leather saddles to calm horses down. One hundred years later, and with no horses in sight, the tradition was still being observed. Whether myth or reality, the story stands as a reminder to question received wisdom.

The Power of Poo

Researchers trying to lessen water contamination in Bolivia have turned to llama dung as a possible remedy. Dung, used in the correct way, has the necessary chemical make-up to neutralize certain acids and dissolve metal content. In Bolivia, run-off from a tin and silver mine has slowly been leaking into the capital city's main water supply. By redirecting the water through "bioreactors" (lagoons and small wetland areas containing the dung), engineers are hopeful that the problem can be sorted out. The citizens of La Paz could soon have fresh, clean water—thanks to a few carefully placed llama droppings.

SCAT FACT

Dried llama dung is often used as fuel, despite the fact that it releases a pungent aroma while being burned. A Peruvian steamboat used in the late 1800s had a 60-horsepower engine that was entirely dung-powered. There are no reports on how it smelled.

▼ **Throughout history, llamas and their dung have proved tremendously useful to humans.**

Dog

Order:	Carnivora
Family:	Canidae
Genus:	*Canis* (species *C. lupus familiaris*)
Distribution:	Worldwide
Habitat:	Domesticated
Diet:	Carnivorous, but will eat plant material

Dogs come in all shapes and sizes, with temperaments to match. Having initially been domesticated as working dogs from packs of wolves and wild dogs, the modern canine largely enjoys a more relaxed life as a pet. Their greater physical and emotional closeness with humans has not led to any greater acceptance of their poop, however—far from it. "Man's best friend" can quickly turn into "man's sworn enemy" whenever shit meets shoe.

MESS FACTOR

4 out of 5

Description

Dog poop is formed of thick, brown cylinders measuring roughly 2 to 3 inches (5 to 7.5 cm) long, which are deposited in segments or in a classic "swirl." Because the dog's diet is rich in meat, its scat has a moist, sometimes runny, texture, and the smell can be very strong. Owners are urged to clean up after their dogs, so to "find" a turd often means accidentally stepping in one.

Poochy Poo

Over recent years, there has been an increased awareness of the health risks posed by dog poo in urban environments. Contact with it can lead to parasitic illnesses such as worms, and rain can

▲ **Coming soon to a sidewalk near you—or not, if the authorities' plans for cleaner streets are successful.**

carry bacteria and toxins from the poo to storm drain outlets, leading to possible contamination of both fish stocks and recreational water supplies. Local authorities now provide special bins, bag dispensers, and heavy fines for those who do not comply with new antifouling laws. Those planning to keep a dog these days must not only consider the responsibility and the cost; they also have to be prepared to put their hand in a plastic bag and scoop up steaming dog shit every day for the next 15 years or so.

The Mess(age)

In 2006, dog poop was employed as part of an "Urban Hazard" campaign against George W. Bush. Tiny flags featuring the American president's face were stuck into piles of poo on pavements in the U.K., France, Germany, and the United States.

Roll With It

One common complaint among dog owners is the amount of other poop their pets apparently enjoy. Some dogs can't get enough of a roll around in a pile of dung from a fox/horse/deer/badger/raccoon/cat/other dog. Theories as to why center on canine hunting origins, whereby the dog would try to conceal its approach by masking its own scent with that of its prey. Evolution, obviously, has yet to catch up.

FOX

Order: Carnivora

Family: Canidae

Genera: Various, including Red (*Vulpes vulpes*) and Arctic (*Alopex lagopus*)

Distribution: Worldwide

Habitat: Various, including forest, prairie, farmland

Diet: Omnivorous, including rodents, insects, fruit, worms, carrion

The fox, of which there are twenty-seven separate species, is known and respected throughout the world. The most common is the red fox, whose adaptable and opportunistic nature has led to a surge in numbers in built-up urban environments. Before this, foxes were seen as primarily woodland animals, with accompanying myths and stories to match. Its scat, however, can reveal a very different story.

MESS FACTOR

3 out of 5

Description

Fox dung is cylindrical in form, measuring up to 0.75 inches (2 cm) in width. Each dropping will usually have a twist of hair at the pointed end. The smell is strong and unpleasant, and the color varies from light brown to black, or even white (a sign that the fox in question has been eating bones). Common components of rural foxes' dung are undigested berries or insects, while that of an urban fox can include scraps of plastic or paper.

On the Trail

Much modern scat analysis takes place in the laboratory, and the account of a 2006 Canadian investigation into how many lemmings were being eaten by foxes sheds some light on one of the processes scientists use when dealing with dried poop. To reduce the scat down to its very essentials, it was dried and then heated in an autoclave, a pressurized sterilizing machine. Having then been washed with light detergent and water, the poop was passed through a fine sieve, which separated out all the component material. The samples were finally dried for two hours at 131°F (55°C). The resulting matter could then be analyzed under a microscope.

Such technology creates a clearer picture of how animals live, and can also address some of the myths that surround them. For the rural red fox, its image in the English countryside can be that of a livestock-grabbing menace. Microscopic analysis of its dung, however, reveals the presence of thousands of *chatae*, tiny scale-like growths that help worms move through soil. The idea that 35 percent of a fox's diet consists of earthworms goes some way to counter the animal's reputation, and, while not denying the threat to chickens and sheep that it poses, such poo-based evidence certainly adds something new to the picture.

NUMBER CRUNCHING

A total of 8,729 fox scats were collected by volunteers as part of the National Fox Survey of Great Britain in 2000.

◀ **A twist of hair forms a kind of extravagant flourish at one end of most fox poo.**

Beaver

Order: Rodentia

Family: Castoridae

Genus: *Castor*; North American (*C. canadensis*), Eurasian (*C. fiber*)

Distribution: Parts of North America, Europe, western Asia

Habitat: Lakes and rivers

Diet: Herbivorous, including water plants, trees, roots

The beaver is one of the largest and heaviest rodents in the world, and is an expert in hydro-engineering and dwelling construction, as evidenced by the complex dam systems it builds. A less common sight in nature is the beaver scat, due to the fact that the animal spends much of its time in or around water. You may want to try snorkeling for one, though this is not advised.

MESS FACTOR

3 out of 5

Description

Deposited in clumps, beaver pellets are cylindrical, measuring up to about 2.3 inches (6 cm) long. It is one of the rare mammals to possess a cloaca (a vent, common in most birds, for both urine and dung excretion). Microorganisms in the beaver's gut break down the plant material into digestible bacterial proteins. The resulting dung is highly fibrous, and so floats easily in water.

When the Chips Are Down

The dung of the Eurasian beaver is playing its part in the animal's survival. Over the last five hundred years, while its North American cousin flourished, the Eurasian beaver population dwindled. Its natural habitat of fresh water and wild meadow

▲ **Usually found floating in water, beaver dung is light, fibrous, and highly toxic.**

has been slowly eradicated by intensive cattle grazing and other agricultural developments. The animal's pelt, meat, and castoreum (its musk-like scent) also made it a target for hunters. By the start of the twentieth century, only seven hundred Eurasian beavers remained.

Since the 1920s, however, beavers have been slowly reintroduced into various European countries. On the plus side, they contribute to a more abundant aquatic ecosystem by increasing the natural variation. On the down side, they also contribute their own environmental damage in terms of tree felling, flooding, and even road subsidence. Successful reintroduction therefore depends on effective management, with animal behavior carefully monitored so as not to upset anyone or anything.

Hence the dung. Once a destructive beaver has been relocated from one area to another, the old stomping ground can be liberally decorated with the scat of an unrelated beaver. Any potential new residents checking it out will soon get the (false) message that the territory is already taken, thanks to the pungent castoreum it holds.

YOU GIVE ME BEAVER

Beaver fever, or giardiasis, is a nasty infection resulting from contact with waterborne beaver dung. Sufferers can look forward to diarrhea, cramps, and vomiting.

Deer

Order: Artiodactyla

Family: Cervidae

Genera: Various, including White-Tailed (*Odocoileus virginianus*) and Fallow (*Dama dama*)

Distribution: Worldwide, except Australia and Antarctica

Habitat: Various, from arctic tundra to tropical rainforest

Diet: Herbivorous

Deer have often held symbolic importance for humans, characterized by three different elements: the cute and flopsy fawn; the protective, nurturing doe; and the proud, antler-wielding stag. The meat tastes quite nice, too. Their dung doesn't figure much in this cultural landscape, yet it certainly plays its part in the survival of both the species itself and the environment in which it lives.

MESS FACTOR

2 out of 5

Description

Compared to some other types, the dung of the deer appears quite innocuous. Made up of small, bullet-shaped pellets, often deposited in clumps, it is composed of fine plant material and smells grassy. It is most likely to be found in their feeding areas. While the pellets look similar in appearance to those of both sheep and rabbits, a deer is likely to produce more.

What You Didn't See in Bambi

Although she has just given birth, the white-tailed doe must still go out and look for food, leaving behind her newborn fawn for up to four hours at a time. The fawn is highly vulnerable at this early stage, and stays hidden from potential predators in long grass or under bushes. Smell can also attract attention, so the fawn holds in any waste until its mother comes back. As it relieves itself upon her return, the doe then eats the poo and pee to mask the aroma and protect the fawn when she goes off again. This process lasts for about a month, until the fawn is old enough to run from trouble at a fast enough pace.

Spreading the Message

Research has shown how important deer dung is in terms of plant distribution. Large fruits eaten by a deer are effectively broken down and digested, though seeds from the plants are often small enough to get passed out in the animal's dung still intact. Because it is a ruminant, the journey taken through the deer's digestive tract is a relatively long one, during which time the nimble deer can have covered quite some distance. The seed is thus dispersed far away from the mother plant, and has an extra bonus of landing in a nice mass of ready-made fertilizer.

◀ **Deer droppings play an important part in the survival of newborn fawns.**

Moose

Order:	Artiodactyla
Family:	Cervidae
Genus:	*Alces* (species *A. alces*)
Distribution:	North America, Scandinavia, north Siberia, Mongolia
Habitat:	Forest, wetland, swamp
Diet:	Herbivorous, including young shoots and leaves, bark, nuts, waterplants

The instantly recognizable moose is the largest member of the deer family, and the male's antlers can measure up to 6.5 feet (2 m) in total width, making them the largest carried by any living mammal. Countries such as Canada, Norway, and Sweden, and the American states of Alaska and Maine, have all adopted the moose as their symbolic animal. Indeed, in Alaska the admiration even extends to the animal's dung—despite the fact that it is somewhat misunderstood.

MESS FACTOR

3 out of 5

Description

Most of the year, moose dung is formed of a series of brown, rounded pellets produced in groups. Each pellet measures about 0.75 inches (2 cm) long. They are fairly compact, hard, and dry. In early spring, however, moose dung can look more like that of a bear, with a more moist consistency and less shape. Unlike bear dung, these moose offerings will be greener and less fibrous.

Poo-venirs

Alaska abounds with tourist souvenirs made of moose dung, including earrings, necklaces, key rings, tie tacks, artwork, and even moose-poop fire

▲ **Moose poo—
Alaskans love it!**

starters and lip balm. The town of Talkeetna holds its Moose Dropping Festival every July, featuring music, sports, stalls, and food. The festival highlight is the grand raffle, the Moose Dropping Drop, in which varnished and numbered moose dung pellets are dropped from the air onto a target, with prizes for those nearest to the bullseye.

Wet 'n' Wild

The popularity of such nugget novelties, however, can cause confusion away from the tourist trail. As mentioned above, the shape and consistency of moose dung can change around early spring. The addition of fresh new shoots to its diet leads to more water in the moose's system, and this in turn leads to wetter dung. Furthermore, as a ruminant, the moose depends on the presence of certain bacteria in its four-chambered stomach in order to process the food effectively via fermentation. A sudden change of diet will temporarily change the gut's chemical make-up, and the bacterial adjustment can take around two weeks, after which it's business as usual. Some Alaskans see the wet splats as worrying evidence of a bear, when it was really just a case of a moose fancying something new from the menu.

WRONG END OF THE STICK

One member of an animal rights organization was outraged when she heard about the Moose Dropping Festival, and subsequently phoned organizers to complain. It took them a while to convince her that it was only the dung getting dropped, and not the moose itself.

Goldfish

Class: Actinopterygii
Order: Cypriniformes
Family: Cyprinidae
Genus: *Carassius* (species *C. Auratus*)
Distribution: Worldwide
Habitat: Ponds and freshwater areas in tropical and subtropical areas; also domestic
Diet: Omnivorous, including plant matter, crustaceans, insects, specialized food

The unassuming goldfish, gently swimming around in a tank, has become a standard symbol of domestic peace and tranquillity. Give it some food, though, and the picture soon turns murky. Goldfish poo is part of a complex biological system that belies the placid imagery, and owners should be aware that keeping a goldfish healthy is not just smooth sailing.

MESS FACTOR

2 out of 5

Description

The lack of a stomach means that the goldfish cannot digest the excess proteins in the food it eats. This leads to a lot of waste, which is expelled through the gills and cloaca (the vent for both fecal and urinary waste). A healthy piece of goldfish poo is short, rather chunky, moist, and is the same color as its food.

Keep It Dirty

However nice it may look, a pristine, scrubbed-down fish tank may not be the perfect home for a goldfish. Because its body produces so much waste, it has developed certain natural resources to combat possible infections—a mini-ecosystem involving a complex cycle of nitrates, nitrites, bacteria, and ammonia. Clean everything away in one go and you rid the tank of the natural defences the goldfish needs. The best way to keep the water clean is by "cycling the tank"—that is, changing only half the water at a time, and changing filters individually, rather than doing them all at once.

Doctor Poo-Little

Monitoring the state of a goldfish's poop is a good way of keeping its health in check. Here is a list of poo conditions, with possible causes:

- Thin, floating = poor diet
- Thick, floating = overfeeding, poor diet
- Thin, white, floating = internal bacterial infection
- Long, thick patches, additional mucus = food fermenting in the fish's belly
- Clear, long = re-absorbed eggs
- Brown, misty water = diarrhea infection

LOST IN TRANSLATION

If you are ever in Japan, and someone says to you (when translated), "Oi, goldfish poo! Leave me alone!" it means that you should give that person some room. Inspired by the trails often seen streaming from a goldfish's cloaca, "goldfish poo" suggests someone who is being unpleasantly clingy.

▼ Caught in the act. Goldfish are not shy when it comes to pooping in public.

Opossum

Order:	Didelphimorphia
Family:	Didelphidae
Genera:	Various; species include Virginia (*Didelphis virginiana*) and Lutrine (*Lutreolina crassicaudata*)
Distribution:	North and South America
Habitat:	Woodland and urban areas
Diet:	Omnivorous, including fruit, nectar, small vertebrates, fish, carrion

One of the quirks of natural-history labeling means that it is easy to confuse the American opossum with the Australian possum, especially as they are both marsupials (pouched animals). The fact that the opossum is sometimes referred to as a 'possum (the apostrophe is important) AND that they are distant relatives, only complicates matters. Even their dung looks similar. Safe to say, if you see one in Australia, it's a possum. In America, it's an opossum. Or a 'possum. Clear?

MESS FACTOR

3 out of 5

Description

The omnivorous diet of the opossum makes its scat less regular than that of other animals. While the dung is dark brown and cylindrical, segments of it are often irregularly sized, and can range from small pellets of about 0.75 inches (2 cm) to longer sausage-like logs of over 2 inches (5 cm). The smell can be quite strong and the texture will differ depending on recent feeds.

Defensive Dung

The Virginia opossum, North America's only marsupial, can fall prey to a number of animals, such as foxes, coyotes, and large owls. When under

threat, the animal will initially snarl to deter its predator, but if this fails, a more elaborate defense is engaged. The opossum's body will go stiff, its tongue will hang from its mouth, its anal glands emit an odor similar to that of rotting flesh, and, as a final touch, it defecates a green-colored liquid over itself. This coma-like state lasts for up to four hours, after which, providing the predator has not seen through the deceit, the opossum revives itself and life carries on. This behavior is sufficiently unique that it has passed into the English language: to "play possum" means to play dead.

▲ Carly Simon's favorite—a nice, steaming pile of opossum poop.

Dangerous Dung

The role played by opossum dung in the spread of parasitic illness is a cause for concern. It has been implicated in certain cases of Chagas' disease, a potentially fatal infection affecting humans, particularly in poor areas of South America. The dung is also known to harbor the parasite that, via transmission through birds and insects, leads to equine protozoal myeloencephalitis (EPM) in horses. While attempts can be made to limit contact between horses and opossums, restricting the movement of birds and insects is virtually impossible.

YOU'RE NOT SO VAIN

In 1975, American singer Carly Simon released an album called *Playing Possum*. The cover featured her lying stiff with her tongue hanging out, emitting a noxious odor, with a green liquid coming from her anus. (Not really.)

Elephant

Order: Proboscidea

Family: Elephantidae

Genera: African (*Loxodonta africana*), Asian (*Elephas maximus*)

Distribution: Sub-Saharan Africa, parts of India, Sri Lanka, Southern China, Southeast Asia

Habitat: Various, including grasslands and forests

Diet: Herbivorous, including grasses, fruits, vegetables, leaves, bark

Whether striding majestically across the open plains of Africa or rumbling through the dense tropical jungles of Southeast Asia, elephants are one of the most awesome sights in nature. And no less awesome are the deposits they leave behind. . . . Elephant droppings are among the easiest to identify—if for no other reason than their sheer scale.

MESS FACTOR

5 out of 5

Description

Elephant dung consists of a number of loosely joined individual lumps, known as *boli* (singular *bolus*). This soft, roundish mass can measure between 1.5 and 6 inches (4 and 15 cm). Due to the fact that elephants digest such a small proportion of the material that they ingest (see opposite), the texture is very fibrous, and droppings will contain observable plant matter such as bark, twigs, and complete seedpods.

Quantity Not Quality

Elephants are, of course, large. And, as you would expect, with a large animal you get correspondingly sizeable droppings. Partly this is an inevitable consequence of the elephants' prodigious diet—an adult will spend up to 16 hours a day eating, during which time it can consume 300 to 600 pounds (140 to 270 kg) of food. However, the size of its droppings is a reflection of the fact that elephants only absorb 40 percent of what they consume. This means that 60 percent of what an elephant puts into its mouth comes straight out the other end, and such poor digestive efficiency explains why the elephant needs to eat so much in the first place.

Pillars of the Community

Elephants are a keystone species in the African landscape. Many animals (including humans) benefit from the presence of elephants: they pull down trees, break up bushes, create salt licks, dig waterholes, and forge trails. Just as important to the local ecosystem are elephant droppings. Baboons and birds pick through dung for undigested seeds and nuts; dung beetles use it to harbor their larvae; termites eat it and often begin construction of their mounds under piles of feces. Plants also benefit: the nutrient-rich manure replenishes depleted soil, and it is a vehicle for seed dispersal. In fact, some seeds will not germinate until they have passed through an elephant's digestive system.

SCAT FACT

Fresh elephant dung is a good indicator of body temperature. The bolus of a healthy elephant should be between 97.5 and 99°F (36 and 37°C).

▼ **The giant of the animal kingdom. Each lump can measure up to 6 inches (15 cm) in diameter.**

Horse

Order: Perissodactyla
Family: Equidae
Genus: *Equus* (species *E. caballus*)
Distribution: Worldwide
Habitat: Various, including forest, prairie, farmland
Diet: Herbivorous, including grasses and other vegetation

Throughout history and throughout the world, the horse's strength, resilience, and speed have been harnessed by humans to be used in areas as diverse as transportation, agriculture, defense, and sport. It is a situation that remains today, in spite of an increased replacement by machinery and technology. Living so close to humans, it is no surprise that uses for its dung are similarly varied.

MESS FACTOR

4 out of 5

Description

The horse is responsible for large, brown, rounded pellets, often partly joined to one another, and deposited in heaps. Undigested hay and grasses may be visible, and the odor is strong when the dung is fresh. They are usually found in feeding areas (though stallions will sometimes deposit them in one place, leading to large piles which act as territorial markers). An average horse will dung about fifteen pellets, or "meadow muffins," a day.

Shit Hot

In the days before gas and electricity, horse dung was used for generating heat, and in various ways and contexts. As with that of other animals,

dried horse dung was burned domestically—and still is in some parts of the world. But the heat created by fermenting the dung itself was also of use, though not as common. Alchemists would often use what would now be seen as scientific methods in their investigations into the natural and the supernatural in their attempts to invoke powers greater than themselves. One of the 12 core alchemical processes they used was called "digestion," which involved steadily heating a substance over a period of days or weeks. Before the days of incubators, horse dung would be compacted around a flask containing the substance, concentrating the heat. Similarly, dung would be used to heat hot beds for growing plants in cold climates, in the way that modern greenhouses can today.

Horse dung is still effectively used to make garden compost. A compost heap can be created by layering dung, nitrogen, leaves, vegetable peelings, grass cuttings, and other green matter. The heap should then be covered and kept moist. Because the dung is light and fibrous, the heat and air generated are encouraged to flow throughout, resulting in a concentration of nutrients that plants love.

▲ In the days before cars, such horsey heaps were common sights (and smells) in larger towns and cities.

SMOKIN'

Genuine Horse Shit cigarettes have been available in Mexico for some years. The packet claims they are "mild, sweet and stable-blended," but smokers claim they taste more like Lucky Strikes under a different name.

Cat

Order:	Carnivora
Family:	Felidae
Genus:	*Felis* (species *F. catus*)
Distribution:	Worldwide
Habitat:	Domesticated
Diet:	Carnivorous, including brand-name cat food, insects, small mammals, birds

The domestic cat has been associated with humans for at least 9,500 years, and yet their killer instinct remains, as anyone forced to deal with a decapitated sparrow in the hallway will testify. "Love me, love my poo" could well be a cat's motto—the price paid for their affection is having to clean up after them.

MESS FACTOR

4 out of 5

Description

Cat dung is formed of a series of long, relatively thin pellets that are usually twisted at one end. They are brown and moist when fresh, drying paler and harder. A cat will often bury its dung with a light layer of earth, and its mainly carnivorous diet means the poo is rich and pungent. Fibrous plant matter can aid digestion, and is sometimes visible in the dung.

Cat Shat That

One perennial problem faced by gardeners in suburban areas throughout the world is how to deal with the unwanted presence of cat poo. As well as the smell, the cat's habit of covering its scat with earth means that nearby beloved plants get uprooted in the process. The dung also carries unwanted diseases such as worms and toxoplasmosis, which has been implicated in some forms of schizophrenia amongst vulnerable groups. Remedies for the problem range from low-tech (orange peel, water pistols, mirrors) to state-of-the-art (security lighting, ultrasonic sound boxes) via eyebrow-raising (lion dung—see next page). As yet, no definitive cure-all has been discovered, and so the list of potential tactics grows ever larger.

No More Shitty Kitty

For those owners turned off by the prospect of getting too close to their cat's scat, the animal can be trained to use the bathroom toilet, as used by humans. Over a period of time, the litter tray should be inched closer to the toilet bowl, then suspended above with the aid of specially manufactured adapters. The cat can then be encouraged to start sitting on the toilet seat. A safety grid that lets the poo pass should also be temporarily installed to prevent the animal from falling in, until such a time as the cat can do everything other than wipe its butt and pull the chain after use.

SCAT FACT

Because of its high protein content, some dogs will readily eat cat poo.

▼ Litter trays bearing nuggets such as these can be found in homes and apartments the world over.

Lion

Order:	Carnivora
Family:	Felidae
Genus:	*Panthera* (species *P. Leo*)
Distribution:	Parts of central and southern Africa, and the Gir Forest, India (the only home of the Asiatic lion)
Habitat:	Open plain, savannah, forest
Diet:	Carnivorous, including large and small mammals, fish, reptiles, amphibians

From the growling beast of the MGM film trailer to the nobility of Aslan, the leonine stand-in for Jesus in C. S. Lewis's Narnia books, the lion has long inspired awe and respect for its standing as one of nature's top predators. As with all animals, its dung bears traces of the life it leads, and as such can prove both nutritional and cautionary.

MESS FACTOR

5 out of 5

Description

Lion dung is made up of quite large, cylindrical segments measuring roughly 4 inches (10 cm) long. These are usually tapered at one end, typical of cat dung. The texture is dense and moist, and may contain traces of a recent meal, such as an impala hoof or zebra hair. Because of the animal's blood-rich diet, lion dung is normally dark brown to black, though it can be white, indicating the presence of calcium through bone ingestion.

Lean, Mean, Pooping Machine

Like most of the big cats, a lion's design is focused on its predatory nature and the climax of the kill. Any excess weight may impede acceleration speed or agility, and such bulk may include food making its way through the digestive system. Lions, therefore, do not digest their kills as efficiently as other animals, resulting in dung that is still relatively high in nutritional value. It is not unusual, then, for scavengers—such as spotted hyenas, hooded vultures, and other animals more able to extract every last ounce of goodness from whatever's going—to help themselves to the odd bit of lion poop.

The Scent of a Lion

Lion dung has proved to be something of a useful substitute when a lion itself is not to hand. "Silent Roar" pellets are made of organic matter soaked in "essence" of lion dung and are designed to be spread on lawns and flower beds to deter domestic cats from ripping them up. In Japan, diluted dung was spread onto a stretch of railtrack that had been plagued by wild deer and raccoons jumping into the paths of trains, causing accidents and delays. The ability of dung to carry with it the marks of its "creator" can thus be put to use, with varying degrees of success.

▼ **Lion scat— good news for scavengers and gardeners, bad news for cats and mounted officers.**

Cougar

Order:	Carnivora
Family:	Felidae
Genus:	*Puma* (species *P. concolor*)
Distribution:	South America and parts of North America
Habitat:	Various, including mountains, forest, grassland, swamps
Diet:	Carnivorous, primarily deer, but also insects and other mammals

The cougar/panther/puma/mountain lion (it has over forty different common names) is solitary, secretive, and primarily nocturnal. Something of a rural myth surrounding the animal has developed, thanks to its fearsome reputation and proximity to certain towns and villages. The myth is compounded by alleged sightings, shaky photographs, tales of screams in the night, inconclusive paw prints, and piles of supposed cougar poop.

MESS FACTOR

4 out of 5

Description

The cougar's dung is often formed of segmented, cylindrical, light brown pellets, similar to that of a coyote or large dog. If the animal has been feeding on the soft internal organs of its prey, however, the dung is likely to be darker and runnier. Traces of hair and fragments of bone are often visible, and the smell is strong. Some 80 percent of cougar dung material is deer-related.

Piles of It

Depending on the food supply, a male cougar's territory can cover a range of over 100 square miles (160 square km), and it is one of many animals to use its scat as a marker of its domain.

The dung will sometimes be deposited and left in the open, but more often the cougar will create what is called a "scrape," which consists of dung and urine—together with soil and other forest litter such as pine needles, leaves, and so on—scraped together into a pile. Scrapes measure at least 3 to 6 inches (10 to 15 cm) high and are left along well-used trails, under trees, along ridges, and near recent kills. Although naturally territorial, a male cougar, on seeing the scrapes of another, will respect these "No Trespassing" signs, and establish its own home range elsewhere. Avoiding the poo means avoiding conflict.

It Was THIS Big . . .

Much confusion can surround the identification of cougar poop, with people believing (or wanting to believe) they have found incontrovertible evidence of an animal on their doorstep. As with the bear, the idea of a wild cat in the vicinity can simultaneously enthral and appall, causing excitement, fear, and a huge rush of life-affirming adrenalin. And when the test results come back negative, as they are likely to do, the flurry may die down. Until the next time . . .

FANCY SCAT

Cougars are kept as pets, both legally and illegally. Owners are recommended to use children's wading pools as litter trays.

Tiger

Order:	Carnivora
Family:	Felidae
Genus:	*Panthera* (species *P. tigris*)
Distribution:	Parts of Asia
Habitat:	Forest, grassland, swamps
Diet:	Carnivorous, including large mammals and reptiles

Another apex predator (one at the top of its food chain), the tiger is the biggest big cat. What it lacks in speed it makes up for in power—when hunting, it can knock its sizeable prey over then follow with a bite to the neck. Such prowess has made it desirable to hunters, and it is now an endangered species. Its dung is being used in the fight for its survival, having previously been used in a very different conflict: the Vietnam War.

MESS FACTOR

5 out of 5

Description

As a solitary and highly territorial animal, the tiger will use dung deposits as range markers, adding urine and anal gland secretions to the pile to reinforce the message. Bearing the characteristics of typical feline dung, it leaves large cylindrical segments that are tapered at one end. Some kind of bone content and hair will be visible, and the tiger's low metabolism means that it may not dung for days.

Sniffer Dogs

On the far eastern coast of Russia, teams of dogs have been trained to sniff out tiger scat. This use of scent dogs has been practiced in various places around the world since the early 1990s, and is handy for a number of reasons: the process is noninvasive and relatively cheap (unlike fitting the animals with transmitters, for instance); the dogs are able to cover a lot of ground; and it's reliable. In Russia, the dogs sniffing out the Amur tiger (*P. tigris altaica*) were able to identify samples from individual animals, enabling researchers back at the lab to analyze their diet and gain a better picture of how tigers use their environment.

Got Dung?

Just as hunters target the tiger for its fur, its claws, and any other valuable piece of the animal, so its dung can be much sought after. Indonesian *Dukuns*, or shamen, believe tiger poo can ward off black magic, with victims treated by ingesting the dung straight from the ground. In traditional Chinese medicine, the dung could be used to treat alcoholism, boils, and hemorrhoids. And, as with that of the lion (see page 44), tiger dung has proved a financial hit when used as a repellent against cats, kangaroos, rabbits, goats, and wild pigs, among others, from gardens and crop fields all over the world.

A-POO-CALYPSE NOW

The CIA developed a radio transmitter disguised as a piece of tiger poo as part of their surveillance armory during the Vietnam War. The transmitter was air-dropped onto the Ho Chi Minh trail, where it could track nocturnal supply movements, safe in the knowledge that no one would pick it up.

▼ **A tapered end is a feature common to the dung of many feline species, as is its use as a territorial marker.**

Gecko

Class: Reptilia
Order: Squamata
Family: Gekkonidae
Genera: Numerous, including House (*Hemidactylus frenatus*) and Tokay (*Gekko gecko*)
Distribution: Equatorial regions worldwide
Habitat: Various, including forest, savannah, urban
Diet: Omnivorous, including insects, small vertebrates, fruit, spiders

Kept as pets or living out in the wild, the sound of them padding around at night eating insects is enough to bring out the creepy-crawlies in some people, yet it is in this role of pest controller that the lizard-like, master-climbing gecko excels. The fact that its droppings can contaminate and stain furniture, carpets, walls, and curtains does little more for its image, and proves enough of a turnoff even for some with a sizeable cockroach infestation.

MESS FACTOR

1 out of 5

Description

A gecko's poop is similar in appearance to that of a mouse, being made up of a series of very small pellets that can measure up to 0.3 inches (1 cm) long, depending on the size of the animal. The droppings are almost totally odorless, quite firm in texture, and should be cleaned immediately from domestic areas.

Ones and Twos

Perhaps the most obvious signifier of a gecko's droppings is the presence of a white tip of sediment at one end. As with birds and most reptiles, the gecko has a cloaca, which is a hole from which the animal secretes all its waste.

▲ **A typical gecko poop next to a pellet of white uric acid. The pellets are small, light, and highly compact.**

The bodies of such animals store and re-use as much water as they can, leading to a more solid, drier form of urine called uric acid, which is then dunged out with the darker feces, and becomes visible as the white flourish. This process of maximizing water extraction is particularly suited to animals—like the gecko—that live in warmer, drier climates.

GOT GECKO POOP?

Spray lemon oil onto a soft cloth and wipe down all window ledges and baseboards. This provides a film that the gecko droppings will sit on rather than seep into. They can then be simply vacuumed off without scrubbing. Magic!

Up Shit Creek

One potentially fatal condition that geckos can be exposed to is that of "impaction," where the animal cannot poop at all. Having consumed an amount of indigestible matter, the gecko's digestive tract becomes blocked, which, if untreated, can prove deadly. In the wild, a common cause is sand or rock particles that are inadvertently eaten along with the animal's prey. Domestically, many substrates (materials used to line a reptile's cage or tank) continue to be made with sand, and so similar situations arise. The safest and cheapest option for any gecko-owner is to line the tank with paper towels or newspaper, completely avoiding any sand-based product.

Giraffe

Order: Artiodactyla
Family: Giraffidae
Genus: *Giraffa* (species *G. camelopardalis*)
Distribution: Southern Africa
Habitat: Dry savannah and open woodland
Diet: Herbivorous, including leaves, twigs, other vegetation

Another one of nature's majesties, the giraffe is loved the world over, despite being geographically limited to the African savannah. With its characteristic markings, long legs, and even longer neck, it is the tallest of all land-living animals and can reach heights of nearly 20 feet (6 m). With such a long way to fall, it's no wonder that giraffe dung breaks up on landing.

MESS FACTOR

3 out of 5

Description

Giraffe poo consists of a number of relatively large pellets (average 1 inch, or 2.5 cm, diameter) that are deposited in groups that scatter. Because the animal extracts as much nutrition as possible from the vegetation it eats (thanks to its four-chambered stomach), the dung texture is quite firm and fibrous. It has a grassy aroma, and each pellet is roughly spherical, usually with a point at one end.

Feeling Gassy

As detailed in the fox section (pages 26–7), scat analysis can be of enormous benefit to scientists trying to gain a clearer picture of animal life. Herbivorous animals present more of a challenge, as their dung is composed of much finer, less easily identifiable material. One recent study in Florida, however, involved converting giraffe dung into gas, having initially freeze-dried it and ground it down. The gas was then analyzed and its structure reported as a sequence of alkanes, or essential chemical compounds. Such information could then be used to determine the real nutritional value of what the giraffe eats, which in turn benefits management of the creatures both in captivity and in the wild.

The Wonder of Poo

Dung contains a lot of information, and zookeepers in Dudley, England, used it in an effort to inspire lust in their male giraffe who had been showing a distinct lack of interest in the zoo's two females. Male giraffe dung was imported from other conservation centers and zoos and laid out in the enclosure to stimulate the male into thinking he had competition for the females' attention. Within a few months, a baby female was born, though as giraffes take fourteen to fifteen months to gestate, they probably need not have bothered.

FANCY A GAME?

Bushmen in the South African savannah like to entertain themselves with a game of giraffe dung spitting.

◄ The higher they come, the harder they fall—giraffe dung pellets scatter on impact.

Chimpanzee

Order: Primate

Family: Hominidae

Genus: *Pan*; species include Common (*P. troglodytes*) and Bonobo (*P. paniscus*)

Distribution: West and central Africa

Habitat: Tropical forest, wet savannah

Diet: Omnivorous, mainly vegetarian (fruit, nuts, leaves), also insects and small mammals

As the closest animal relative to humans, the common chimpanzee has been the subject of many behavioral and biological investigations. Qualities we see in ourselves can be easily identified among their similarly complex social structures. The scientific examination of their dung has also led to some surprising results.

MESS FACTOR

3 out of 5

Description

Chimp dung is usually found by pathways, and its appearance will reflect its depositor's diet. It can contain whole undigested leaves and seeds, as well as large amounts of hair (from grooming).

The Appliance of Science

In 1995, biologist Jane Goodall observed the presence of a number of undigested *Aspilia* leaves in chimp dung. Further research has shown that these hairy leaves have an almost Velcro-like effect on parasitic worms living in the ape's gut, clearing the worms off and keeping them off until they are dumped out the rectum. The leaves have no known nutritional value, and such behavior is indicative of the chimp's ability to self-medicate.

A pile of chimp dung on the floor in Oklahoma led to the culprit demonstrating a facility to lie. "Lucy Temerlin" was an ape living in a primate study institute, and was taught sign language as a means to investigate how chimps learn and communicate. Having pooped, the animal was then asked if she was responsible. She signed back that she wasn't, and instead blamed a graduate student working there, then her interviewer. She finally admitted to lying, and apologized, but researchers were struck by how the chimp had demonstrated a high degree of self-awareness.

A more sinister side of the close human/chimp relationship was revealed in 2006, when chimp dung provided vital clues in establishing the origin of the Human Immunodeficiency Virus that causes AIDS. Scientists found feces among a chimp population in southeast Cameroon in west Africa that contained SIV, an ape-related strain of the virus. It is thought that SIV was passed on to humans in the early twentieth century through the local trade in ape meat. While apparently harmless to the apes, the virus mutated in its human form to create a global pandemic that now affects some forty million people.

▲ **Often bearing traces of their last meal, chimp poop reveals much about the animal and its wider world.**

SCAT FACT

While chimps in captivity can be coprophagous (that is, they'll eat their own poo), no such behavior has ever been recorded in the wild.

Seagull

Class: Aves
Order: Charadriiformes
Family: Laridae
Genera: Various; species include Common (*Larus canus*), Herring (*L. argentatus*), and Kittiwake (*Rissa tridactyla*)
Distribution: Worldwide
Habitat: Various
Diet: Omnivorous, including garbage

Strictly speaking, there is no "seagull"—the word has no fixed meaning in the field of biological naming, and the birds in question are, technically, just "gulls." This technical point is, of course, unlikely to be of interest to anyone whose stroll along the beach is interrupted by a streak of (sea)gull shit landing on their head. The presence of opportunistic seagulls can cause headaches for some civic beachside authorities, though recent research suggests much darker consequences regarding the radioactivity of certain bird poop samples.

MESS FACTOR

3 out of 5

Description

Seagull droppings are a combination of feces and uric acid, ejected through the bird's cloaca. They are usually white (the uric acid), and sometimes contain black islands (the feces), though the color can vary depending on diet. They are moist and runny when fresh, and dry to leave a chalky residue that can stain due to its high acidity.

Toxic Shock

As with mice and rats, the fact that seagulls live so close to humans, and have developed a taste for garbage, has led to their developing a reputation for being a pest. The germs and diseases they pick up scavenging can easily be pooped into aquatic areas used for drinking water or leisure and recreation. DNA tests have identified seagull droppings as a primary source of *E. coli* bacteria in certain areas, and they have been implicated in outbreaks of chlamydia, salmonella, and other fungal and bacterial infections. Diseases such as bird flu could also also be transmitted because of the birds' migration patterns, although apportioning blame without hard evidence is as much about guesswork as it is hard science.

In 1998, managers suggested to their workers at Sellafield nuclear plant in England that they wear protective clothing when working outside, as seagull droppings from the area had been found to be radioactively contaminated. In 2003, researchers in the Arctic similarly found evidence of unusually high levels of radioactive material in the dung (guano) of several bird species, including gulls, which was attributable to the Chernobyl disaster and earlier nuclear weapons testing. These high levels are not just problematic for the birds; whole ecosystems can be affected and depleted, the problem being compounded again by the gulls' migratory habits.

PRICE OF POOP

In 2006, an English seagull that dive-bombed a diner's lunch and pooped all over it paid the ultimate price. The diner's husband shot it dead with an air rifle.

▼ **The scavenged diet of the seagull means that its poop carries more toxins than that of other more finicky birds.**

Rabbit

Order: Lagomorpha	

Order: Lagomorpha

Family: Leporidae

Genera: Various, including European or Afrcan (*Oryctolagus cuniculus*), cottontail (genus *Sylvilagus*)

Distribution: Worldwide, except Antarctica

Habitat: Various, including deserts, grasslands, woodland, coastal plains

Diet: Young woody stems, herbaceous, plants, grasses

They may be small, but there are a lot of them, and rabbits make an ideal subject for novice dropping-spotters. Because they feed on much the same type of food, herbivores such as rabbits, hares, and even deer all have similar droppings. However, close inspection of shape and size will give away the species.

MESS FACTOR

2 out of 5

Description

Rabbit droppings are found in small clusters. In terms of shape and form, individual droppings are generally spherical, around 0.2 to 0.5 inches (5 to 12 mm) in diameter, and composed mostly of undigested fiber. Dark brown and slightly moist when fresh, they dry to a pale dusty color. The odor is slight, but concentrated deposits can give off a smell of ammonia.

Second Bite of the Cherry

Like most lagomorphs—and some types of rodent, including guinea pigs—rabbits actually produce two types of fecal matter: the ordinary pellets as described above, and "cecotropes." The latter are also known as "night feces," as this is the time of day at which they are generally produced.

Smaller, softer, darker, and more moist than the hard fecal pellets, cecotropes are also covered with greenish mucus that makes them clump together. A further difference is the rather pungent odor, which is due to the fact that cecotropes contain a large mass of bacteria.

Cecotropes weren't included under the "Description" heading simply because you are unlikely to find them in the wild. Why? Because rabbits eat them . . . often directly from their anus.

In fact, cecotropes are an essential part of a rabbit's diet, providing vital nutrients and beneficial forms of bacteria, and rabbits deprived of their cecotropes will ultimately succumb to malnutrition. They contain half of the fiber of the typical hard fecal pellet (making it easier for nutrients to be absorbed), and high vitamin levels.

The process by which cecotropes are produced is called "hindgut fermentation." Food passes through the esophagus, stomach, small intestine (where nutrients are absorbed), and then into the colon. It is then consumed and digested for a second time. In this respect, hindgut fermentation is similar to ruminant animals chewing the cud.

BREEDING LIKE RABBITS

In 1859, farmer Thomas Austin released twelve pairs of rabbits on his land in Victoria, Australia. By the late 1940s, their numbers had increased to an estimated 600 million—with catastrophic effects on the country's native fauna and flora.

◀ **An example of the more usual, harder rabbit pellets. Softer cecotropes are harder to find.**

Kangaroo

Order: Diprotodontia
Family: Macropodidae
Genus: *Macropus* (four species)
Distribution: Australia
Habitat: Desert and woodland
Diet: Herbivorous, including grass and roots

The bouncing kangaroo is an animal immediately associated with its native country, and is as much a part of Australian heritage as corked hats and the Sydney Opera House. It is the world's largest living marsupial (pouched mammal), and the red kangaroo can leap to a height of 10 feet (3 m). While interaction with their dung is all part of growing up for kangaroos themselves, humans have been finding other, more lucrative, uses for it.

MESS FACTOR

3 out of 5

Description

The kangaroo is one of the few mammals with a cloaca, and as such it defecates and urinates simultaneously. The kangaroo leaves a group of four to eight dark brown, oval pellets in any one sitting. The dung is similar to that of their close relative the wallaby, but is identifiable by its fine texture (wallaby dung tends to be rougher because the wallaby eats woody plants). The strong, plant-like odor fades over time.

Mother Love

Once born, a joey (baby kangaroo) can stay in its mother's pouch for up to eleven months before it is ready to venture out into the world. It will feed, as most babies do, on its mother's milk, and pees and poos as most babies do, too. To keep the pouch clean, the mother eats whatever waste the joey passes. It will also lick the joey's cloaca area after feeding to stimulate waste disposal and prevent constipation and kidney problems that might otherwise arise from its sedentary life.

Where There's Muck...

Having been inspired by similar enterprises in Africa and Scandanavia, which used elephant and elk poo respectively, a company on the Australian island of Tasmania has started producing paper made from kangaroo dung. The poo is washed, mixed, and then boiled, thus creating the fibers necessary to make "Roo Poo Paper." Customers can choose from a wide range of paper-based products, including journals, cards, photo albums, and writing sets. The paper doesn't smell, but individual bush-grass fibers that were once sitting in dung are visible. And if that whets your appetite, why not invest in a kangaroo-poo paperweight, available from a different but equally scatologically minded company?

▼ **Kangaroo dung is mostly laid in clumps, though it can sometimes be found in unsegmented cylinders, too.**

Mouse

Order: Rodentia
Family: Muridae
Genus: *Mus*; thirty-eight species, including Common House (*M. Musculus*)
Distribution: Worldwide, except Antarctica
Habitat: Various, including buildings, forests, deserts, swamps
Diet: Omnivorous, including insects, worms, carrion, household objects

Like their relatives, the rats, mice are not one of the best-loved of creatures. Their opportunistic nature and potential for carrying disease has made them unwelcome guests in many homes and businesses. The presence of their droppings can shut down a restaurant in minutes—and yet, in Thailand, mouse shit gives a real kick to a curry.

MESS FACTOR

2 out of 5

Description

Narrow, cylindrical, and very small, the mouse's dung pellets are about 0.25 inches (1 cm) long. They contain fine, powdery particles of plant material, pollen grains, insect fragments, or whatever else the mouse has eaten. The smell can be quite strong, and they are either dark brown or black. Easily confused with bat or rat droppings, mouse droppings are usually found near runways, nest and burrow entrances, or in dark corners.

The Disease...

As well as being associated with salmonella and arenavirus, mouse droppings have increasingly come to be seen as dangerous due to the identification and subsequent spread of hantavirus.

In 1993, this virus was linked to the potentially fatal Hantavirus Cardiopulmonary Syndrome (HCPS or HPS), and was found to be carried by rodents' feet and in their urine and droppings. Hantavirus is spread through the air, so the general idea when cleaning up mouse droppings is to wet them with disinfectant or bleach solution before cleaning them away. Droppings shouldn't be swept or vacuumed, as this increases the risks of disturbing the viral spores and of them traveling up your nostrils. However, as is so often the case with new viruses, a lot of panic is generated around what can essentially be tackled with common sense.

...and the Cure?

As much as mice cause disease, they continue to play their part in preventing it, in terms of being used and monitored in laboratories. Lab mice are exposed to various diseases, treated with new drugs to test for safety, and so on, and their droppings play an essential part in the process. Feces reveal a great deal, particularly with modern technology, and rigorous monitoring yields useful information. That some researchers in such institutions spend their days looking at shit may be a small grain of comfort to those who oppose their methods.

ONLY JOKING

"Mouse shit" is indeed used in Thai cooking, but only as a nickname for a kind of chile. Phrik khii nuu chiles are long, thin, and small (hence the name), and are incredibly fiery.

◁ **Very small but potentially deadly, inhaling fumes from mouse droppings should be avoided at all times.**

Rat

Order:	Rodentia
Family:	Muridae
Genus:	*Rattus*; over fifty species, including Black (*R. rattus*) and Brown (*R. norvegicus*)
Distribution:	Worldwide
Habitat:	Various, including coastal, forest, urban
Diet:	Omnivorous, including leaves, cereal, small mammals, birds, detritus

As mammals go, the rat must be one of the least revered. Like its close relative the mouse, its presence can inspire panic and fear, but the rat doesn't have cute and smart Mickey, Jerry, or Stuart Little on its side. While it is certainly true that "Satan's lapdog" damages food supplies, gnaws through cables, and spreads disease, its creativity, resourcefulness, and intelligence are to be admired, as the many people who keep them as pets will agree. And did you ever learn anything about the history of the planet from the crap of Speedy Gonzales?

MESS FACTOR

2 out of 5

Description

A rat will deposit around 50 droppings a day. Each measures approximately 0.5 inches (12 mm) long, has blunt ends, and will be found in the animal's feeding or resting areas. They are dark brown or black, and fresh droppings look wet and have a putty-like consistency. The color fades to gray with time, and the texture becomes more brittle.

Fatal Feces

It is often said that rat droppings are responsible for plague, the disease that in epidemic form killed millions of Asians and Europeans over hundreds

▲ **As rat droppings age, they become drier and more brittle, like these.**

of years during the last millennium. Although this is wrong, their waste is known to transmit diseases such as salmonella, murine typhus fever, and trichinosis. A whole industry is devoted to rat control, encompassing a wide range of products for reducing a rat population and then keeping it in check. Its droppings are a giveaway clue of its presence, and can lead the animal to its death via rodenticide baits, tracking powders, fumigants, glue boards, snap traps, and so on.

Shit House

Pack rats are found in the western United States and northern Mexico, where they create elaborate nests known as middens. One of the main materials they use is their dung, packed around a range of leaves, bark, roots, and so on. The rats urinate over the nest as it's built, helping to strengthen and preserve the materials used via crystallization. Most often found in caves and other sheltered desert areas, matter collected from these nests can be seen in much the same way as fossils. Middens are essentially accumulations of dung, sometimes hundreds of years old—and given the nature of their construction, they also contain flora and fauna from their locality, some of which can date back forty thousand years.

A LOAD OF SHIT

Rat droppings were once seen as a surefire remedy for constipation. And when mixed with honey and lemon juice, they were also used to cure baldness.

Badger

Order:	Carnivora
Family:	Mustelidae (3 subfamilies)
Genera:	Various, including Eurasian (*Meles meles*) and American (*Taxidea taxus*)
Distribution:	Europe, some parts of North America, Africa, Asia
Habitat:	Forest or grassland
Diet:	Omnivorous, including earthworms, insects, small mammals, fish, fruit

The nocturnal badger, with its characteristic striped face, has a long and varied history of interaction with humans. Badger baiting and hunting was, and in some parts of the world still is, a popular blood sport, and the animal has made numerous appearances in both adult and children's literature. Interaction with its poop, however, has added another facet to its personality—that of nuisance.

MESS FACTOR

4 out of 5

Description

Like many animals, the dung of the badger often reflects what it has been eating as part of a very varied diet. A particularly muddy stool suggests a meal of earthworms, the presence of shiny wing casings suggests beetles, and so on. The color will vary accordingly. Being relatively thin and cylindrical, and measuring around 1.5 inches (4 cm), badger dung resembles that of a dog. Found in clumps, it does not have a strong smell.

Dump Dumps

While some badgers are solitary, others live in groups, or clans, and a good indicator of clan activity is a communal toilet. Otherwise known as latrines, they are usually shallow, uncovered areas of earth containing a fair bit of poop. Plants such as elder and nettle love the nitrogenous components released into the soil by the decomposing dung, and so thrive in these areas. Latrines are often found on the boundaries of badger territory, and as such carry a message of communal strength to potential rivals.

TB or Not TB?

The poop of the Eurasian badger has become a sworn enemy of many farmers, especially those in Britain, given its suspected role in the spread of bovine TB, a potentially deadly form of tuberculosis in cows. The badger is a "vector species" (host) of the disease, and cattle can become infected through exposure to the badger's dung (or breath or urine). Badger culls would please the farmers, but outrage environmental groups and the wider British public, as the animal is a protected species. The government faces a problem: how do you persuade a badger to poop in a particular place?

▶ **Seen either on its own or in a larger communal latrine, badger poop closely resembles that of the dog.**

Otter

Order: Carnivora

Family: Mustelidae

Genera: Various; species include Sea (*Enhydra lutris*) and European (*Lutra lutra*)

Distribution: North America, southern Africa, Europe, parts of South America and Asia

Habitat: Rivers, lakes, oceans

Diet: Carnivorous, including fish, some amphibians, shellfish

The otter, like the beaver, is another animal enjoying something of a renaissance, having previously had its habitat threatened by intensive farming methods and its life threatened by hunting. Numerous reintroduction projects are helping to restore the otter back to the streams, rivers, and oceans where it once thrived, and its dung is proving to be a valuable tool in assessing the programs' successes.

MESS FACTOR

3 out of 5

Description

Dark and wet, an otter's dung varies in size according to the individual species responsible. It is generally formed of cylindrical segments, tapered at one or both ends and measuring roughly 1.5 to 3 inches (4 to 7.5 cm) long. Each log, or spraint, will bear traces of the otter's diet, including fish scales, bones, and shellfish casings. The dung will often smell quite strong.

Poop Sleuths

Some species of otter, like the European, will dung in prominent places such as on boulders, and may use the same individual spot time and time again. As with other animals, this serves a territorial purpose. Other species such as the South American giant otter (*Pteronura brasiliensis*), however, establish a communal toilet area called a latrine, which will be used by all otters in the area.

Surveys of otter spraints have proved highly effective in determining population growth and distribution. Latrines are particularly useful because their size, giveaway fishy smell, and conspicuous locations all make them easier to spot. The dung's acidity also means that any underlying grass or vegetation in the latrine tends to turn yellow and die off—another handy signpost.

Investigating individual spraints can also yield highly useful information, especially when compared to more traditional tracking methods such as telemetry, whereby the otter would be fitted with a small radio transmitter. Telemetry was only as effective as the strength of the battery used, and the devices would start to fail after about a year. DNA profiling gained from spraint deposits is less invasive, and means that individual otters can be identified and monitored over several years, leading to a greater understanding of how the animals use their particular habitats, how they eat, how they interact with each other, and so on.

SCAT FACT

An otter's fast metabolism and highly active nature mean that it must eat up to 15 percent of its body weight in food every day—which makes for a lot of spraints.

▼ **An otter poop, or spraint. Within this beauty lies a whole range of information about the animal responsible.**

Aardvark

Order: Tubulidentata
Family: Orycteropodidae
Genus: *Orycteropus* (species *O. afer*)
Distribution: Central and southern Africa
Habitat: Dry savannah, rainforest
Diet: Omnivorous, mainly termites but also other insects and cucurbit fruit (*Cucumis humifructus*)

The secretive, nocturnal aardvark is perhaps best known, in English-speaking countries at least, for having the name that kick-starts most encyclopedias. Having developed a quite touching dung-centered relationship with a particular cucumber-like fruit, however, the animal has also found fame and appreciation amongst African botanists.

MESS FACTOR

2 out of 5

Description

Aardvark dung is made up of a number of small oval pellets containing organic matter, termite casings, and seeds. They are 0.5 to 0.75 inches (1.2 to 2 cm) in diameter and are deposited in hollows dug about 4 inches (10 cm) deep. The dung, which has a light smell of ammonia when fresh, is then covered over with a layer of earth. These hollows are found near aardvark lairs, along trails, or in feeding areas.

Bum Deal

The aardvark's main source of nutrition is the termite. Having the strength to dismantle a termite mound with its powerful claws, it uses its snout and long thin tongue that's covered with thick sticky saliva to root out the insects in vast numbers, aided by nostrils that can open and shut at will. Once out the other end, the termite remains are buried, perhaps to disguise the giveaway ammonia fumes from more unsuspecting insects in the vicinity.

Another reason why they bury their dung can be attributed to their fruitier foodstuff. Aardvarks are the only animal known to feed on the cucurbit fruit, and as such appear to be crucial to its survival. Living in hot, dry climates, the aardvark relies on the fruit as a welcome source of water. The cucurbit's undigested seeds get passed out in the aardvark's dung, landing back outside in a rich steaming pile of free fertilizer. That the aardvark then covers this pile with a light layer of earth suggests that it is re-planting the seeds in the knowledge that they will soon grow into more thirst-quenching cucurbits. It's an almost symbiotic relationship that has led the fruit to become known locally as the "aardvark cucumber," and is the only plant in its family to be grown underground. Without the poop, it, and maybe the aardvark, would be pooped.

▼ **Aardvarks bury their dung both to mask the smell and to encourage the growth of their favorite fruit.**

Koala

Order: Diprotodontia
Family: Phascolarctidae
Genus: *Phascolarctos* (species *P. cinereus*)
Distribution: Eastern coast of Australia
Habitat: Forests and woodland
Diet: Herbivorous, mainly eucalyptus leaves

Another great Australian symbol, the koala, spends most of its time sleeping in trees. Its name is possibly derived from the Aboriginal meaning "no drink," and it is true that most if not all of the liquid refreshment they need comes from the copious quantities of eucalyptus leaves they eat. The sight of a koala with its young in a tree has certainly got the "ahhhh" factor, but be prepared to read something that might make you go "uurrrghhh."

MESS FACTOR

2 out of 5

Description

The hard, firmly packed pellets of koala dung are usually long and cylindrical, with a slightly ridged surface. They are brown, and, unsurprisingly, contain fragments of eucalyptus leaf. They even smell of eucalyptus oil when fresh, and are likely to be found on the ground underneath the trees that the koalas occupy.

Pappy Love

The koala feeds on the leaves of about twenty species of eucalyptus, and very little else. The leaves typically contain toxic oils, little nitrogen, and 50 percent water, but the animal's digestive system is well prepared to deal with this relatively

poor diet. The liver will neutralize the toxins, while, further on, hindgut fermentation in the enlarged cecum enables microbes to digest the plant's cellulose, a substance that mammals find notoriously difficult to break down, This process is similar to that in rabbits (see pages 58–9), but, unlike them, koalas don't have to reingest any waste, as the cecum is large enough to do the job of re-absorption, which keeps things tidy.

Young koalas do not get away so lightly. Because they are not born with all the bacteria and chemicals necessary for efficient digestion, the mother, while weaning, produces a particular kind of soft feces called "pap," which she feeds the joey while it is still in its pouch. Pap contains high levels of protein, B vitamins, vitamin K, minerals, volatile fatty acids, fungi, and bacteria to boost the joey's immune system and equip it for all it needs in later life. Eating the pap makes the joey stronger, enabling it to make the move from milk to eucalyptus.

▲ **Koala pellets are long and cylindrical, and are a must-have souvenir for any self-respecting tourist in Australia.**

BAG OF SHITE

Gunnedah, a town north of Sydney, has a famously large koala population. Tourists can buy their very own bag of koala dung to take home as a memento of their stay in "The Koala Capital of the World."

Seal

Order:	Carnivora
Family:	Phocidae, Otariidae
Genera:	Various, including Monk (*Monachus monachus*) and Gray (*Halichoerus grypus*)
Distribution:	Both polar regions, parts of Europe, Africa, America, Australia
Habitat:	Shores and coastal areas
Diet:	Carnivorous, including krill, fish, squid, other seals

The seal is a large marine mammal adapted to life both on land and in the sea, although the former makes them a lot more vulnerable to predators—and especially humans. Hunters kill the animals, mainly for their pelts and meat, and animal rights protesters have adopted their cause with conviction. Hence, seals are one of the more controversial of animals, and even their feces can figure in some lively debates.

MESS FACTOR

3 out of 5

Description

Seals deposit large, roughly cylindrical segments similar to dog poop, that contain bone fragments and other dietary remnants. These set to a concrete-like hardness when dry. They can also produce soft, wet, shapeless dung if they've been eating soft-bodied animals. The smell is strong and unpleasant, and they defecate either at haul-out sites or (most often) in the water itself.

Fecal Fossils

Similar to the preservative qualities of pack-rat middens, seal dung has been investigated for its archeological properties. Poop samples collected from the sea-bed sediment in Antarctica contain

The seal-versus-human debate has been played out on a more local level in San Diego, where a colony of seals has established itself at an open-air swimming pool. For: those who find the creatures cute and of scientific interest. Against: those who can't stand the smell of the built-up mounds of seal dung.

▼ **Controversial poop from a controversial animal—seal scat has both good and bad sides.**

traces of seal hair, which in turn contains keratin and other non-perishable elements that reflect the chemical make-up of the surrounding environment. The dung can be dated, as can its metalloid contents such as mercury, copper, and cadmium, opening the door for archeological investigation by way of natural science.

They're Good! They're Bad!

Increases in seal populations, thanks to improved conservation, have not always been greeted with enthusiasm. Fishermen claim that the prevalence of the seal has led to damaging depletion of fish stocks. As well as eating the fish for themselves, parasites carried in the animal's feces can damage them, too. In Nova Scotia, for example, cod-worm eggs pass into the marine food chain via the seal's poop. Through a complex network of other vector (host) invertebrate species, the parasite eventually infects the flesh of the fish. It is also resistant to freezing, and can be rejuvenated by the cooking process, which hardly makes for the nicest supper. Those on the other side of the argument claim that hunting and culling seals has a relatively small impact on fishing stocks. And so the arguments trundle on.

Rhinoceros

Order: Perissodactyla

Family: Rhinocerotidae

Genera: Various; species include Black (*Diceros bicornis*) and White (*Ceratotherium simum*)

Distribution: Eastern and southern Africa, some regions of Asia

Habitat: Various, including desert, grassland, forest, savannah

Diet: Herbivorous, including grass, leaves, fruit

The rhinoceros uses its distinctive horn when guarding its territory, fighting rivals, protecting its young and shoveling earth. The horn is, however, not a true one, being instead made of thick, matted hair that is separate from its skull. Its dung, on the other hand, is real and is proving to be of some use in staving off the dangers of extinction for this, one of the world's most critically endangered animals.

MESS FACTOR

4 out of 5

Description

The rhino dispatches large, heavy, bar-like dung that is brown when fresh. Because of its herbivorous diet, the dung is fibrous and compact. It is possible to detect differences in species due to differences in the poo—the black rhino's tends to be more woody thanks to the larger amount of tougher vegetation it consumes. A rhinoceros will often deposit its dung in a communal latrine.

Bowel Movements

The acute sense of smell that rhinos enjoy enables them to pick up on valuable information stored in their dung, such as a male's status within a group or a female's reproductive condition, and

▲ **Rhinos, like many animals, are not averse to the odd spot of poop-munching.**

this obviously has a further effect in terms of behavior and population growth. Given this keen sensitivity, biologists involved in population management of rhinos have used dung as part of relocation programs. Relocation is not a simple exercise—it stresses the animals, which can then lead to infighting, accidents, injury, and ultimately even death. Similarly, if part of a group is relocated, those left behind are often wary about spreading out into the newly vacated areas. Strategic dung placement in both old and new territories can help rhinos overcome initial fears, and instill greater confidence until such a time as they have happily re-established themselves.

Dung can also be used in another way of easing the trauma of relocation. In southern Africa, groups of black and white rhinoceros have been moved around different large wildlife reserves in an effort to boost numbers. Dung samples are taken and analyzed at various stages of the operation, primarily to monitor the animals' hormone levels, which are reliable stress indicators. Thus, as with many other endangered animals, the poop of the rhino is being used in attempts to secure them a stronger future.

FOR THE GAR-DUNG . . .

A New Zealand company (www. endangeredfaeces. co.nz) aims to help save the rhino while improving your roses. Their rhino-poop compost is shaped like the animal (not life-size). Just place in the garden, add water, and the nitrogen-rich statue slowly dissolves into the soil.

Dung Beetle

Class: Insecta
Order: Coleoptera
Family: Scarabaeidae
Genera: Various, with some 7,000 separate species
Distribution: Worldwide, except Antarctica
Habitat: Various, including forest, desert, grassland
Diet: Coprophagous (dung eater)

Strictly speaking, the dung beetle should not be in this book, for it is not its own poop that is of interest, but rather what it does with that of other animals. The dung beetle loves the stuff—living in it, eating it, breeding in it—and it doesn't seem too fussy about whose end it came from—elephant, cow, monkey, horse, kangaroo, llama . . .

MESS FACTOR

1 out of 5

Meet the Family

There are essentially three kinds of dung beetle: house-hunters, tunnelers, and rollers. The house-hunter is relatively small and will burrow inside the dung, eating and resting accordingly. The tunneler is slightly larger and chooses to bury itself in a passage underneath the piece of dung. At the end of this passage, it will store a mound of dung, excavated from above, inside of which the female will then lay eggs. Once the eggs have hatched, the dung provides the larvae with all the nutrients they need. The third type of dung-beetle, the roller, makes a ball of dung (often much larger than itself), and rolls it away to a quieter spot to either feed on or mate in. In the case of the latter, both male and female create the ball, and sometimes perform poop gymnastics as the male pushes it along with its legs while the female rides on top in their search for a suitable resting point. As with the tunneler, the roller will go on to lay its eggs inside the ball.

Back to Nature

Dung beetles don't hang about—whereas one cow chip may last up to four years in a field without any intervention, it will disappear within two days at the hands (or rather legs) of a band of dung beetles. The processes they use break down and aerate the dung, and once it is buried the surrounding soil is fertilized.

The speed with which dung beetles operate also means that the larvae of other, more destructive insects that feed off dung bacteria, such as flies, don't have time to establish themselves. Dung beetles have thus been imported to countries like Australia to successfully control and/or prevent infestations of such creatures.

HOT SHIT

The dung beetle, rolling its ball of dirt along the ground, was seen by the ancient Egyptians as a mirror image of the sun as it daily rolls across the sky. They therefore venerated the beetle and its depiction is rife in art from that period.

◀ A roller getting nimble with a small ball of fresh elephant dung. Larger balls are often made, too.

Penguin

Class: Aves
Order: Sphenisciformes
Family: Spheniscinae
Genera: Various, including Crested (*Eudyptes*) and Great (*Aptenodytes*)
Distribution: Antarctica, southern parts of Australia, Africa, South America
Habitat: Oceans, coasts
Diet: Carnivorous, including krill, fish, squid

The black-and-white penguin has come to be widely loved by humans. A polar animal, it lives in a land that lies on the frontline of discussions about climate change, and films and television programs for adults and children alike have further popularized its appeal. Recent research into penguin dung, or guano, has led to some surprising results that Morgan Freeman certainly never told you about.

MESS FACTOR

3 out of 5

Description

Penguin guano has a strong, fishy odor, and its color reflects what the bird has been eating—white or grey from fish, pink from krill; yellow from squid, and green from algae (or if the bird has been living off the built-up reserves in its stomach). The guano is moist and runny, and can be ejected from the bird's cloaca with such force that it will hit other nearby penguins.

Piling High

Penguins gather in large groups, or colonies, which can number over a million birds of certain species. The corresponding build-up in guano, however, is not without problems. The financial value of guano as a nitrogen-rich fertilizer led to extensive harvesting of colonies of black-footed penguins (*Spheniscus demersus*) in South Africa. The birds there used to excavate their nests in the sun-hardened dung, so when it was gone, they had to brood under bushes or create surface nests, which made them more vulnerable to predators. Further south, accumulations of dung up to 3 feet (1 m) high threatened to destroy the first dwelling ever built in Antarctica. Thanks to a renovation appeal, though, it appears a poop-free future for the building has been secured.

Ready, Aim ... Fire!

As mentioned above, certain penguins are capable of propelling their guano far from the point of defecation. Brooding birds, particularly, have been observed doing this, possibly to avoid soiling the nest at their feet. Having maneuvered themselves to the edge of the nest, with their cloacas pointing outwards, both Chinstrap (*Pygoscelis antarctica*) and Adelie (*P. adeliae*) penguins will let fly a streak of guano that can land up to 16 inches (40 cm) away, over time creating a radial pattern.

ANYONE FOR A SPLAT?

A Penguin in the U.K. is a kind of chocolate-covered cookie. In 2003, the manufacturer released two new products— Penguin Splatz and Penguin Mini-Splatz (bite-size version). They have since been discontinued.

▼ **Because of the penguin's defecatory habits, an aerial view of its nest will resemble the spokes of a bicycle wheel.**

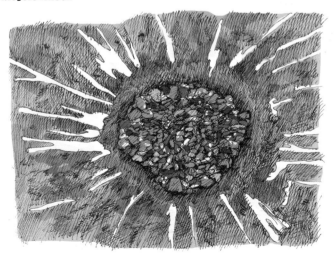

Owl

Class: Aves

Order: Strigiformes

Family: Strigidae (typical owls) and Tytonidae (barn owls)

Genera: Various, including *Asio* (eared owls) and *Bubo* (eagle owls)

Distribution: Worldwide, except Antarctica

Habitat: Various, including forest, prairie, polar

Diet: Carnivorous

Having long been a focus for myth-makers and storytellers, the solitary, nocturnal owl is both feared and revered throughout the world. As with a number of other birds (such as eagles, herons, crows, and most other raptors), the owl is responsible for two types of waste product—pellets and droppings. Although the former does not strictly fall into the fecal category, it is of sufficient interest to warrant a mention here, and so the pellet becomes, temporarily, an honorary turd.

MESS FACTOR

3 out of 5

Description

Owl droppings are similar to those of other birds. A combination of uric acid and feces, they are dunged from its common vent, the cloaca, and are usually white in color. They are produced in considerable volume, and this has earned them the nickname "whitewash." Pellets, on the other hand, are released through the mouth. These vary in size (from 0.5 to 4 inches, or 1.2 to 10 cm, long) and are dark in color, later fading to grey. Pellets contain indigestible matter from the owl's diet, such as bones, fur, and feathers. Both waste products are found around the base of trees where the bird has been eating.

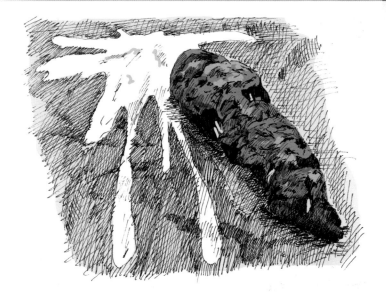

In and Out, Up and Down

The stomach of an owl is composed of two parts. Food enters the first (the glandular stomach, or "crop") and is initially broken down by enzymes, acids, and mucus. The second part (the muscular stomach, or "gizzard") is a kind of filter, containing small, rounded pieces of grit that act like teeth on the harder bits of food. Insoluble matter such as bone and fur is held back here, while the soluble materials pass on through the rest of the intestine to be ejected as droppings through the cloaca. Back in the gizzard, the detritus that remains is compressed into a pellet (also called a "casting"), which then travels back up to the crop, where it can stay for up to ten hours. When the owl needs to vacate the crop to make room for another fresh meal, the original pellet is coughed up and ejected. So, if you catch an owl throwing up, it means it's hungry.

▲ **Pellets contain the bone fragments and other indigestible elements that cannot make it through as "whitewash."**

SCAT FACT

Owl pellets contain more fragments than those of other birds, for two reasons. First, the owl's digestive juices are not as strong. Second, it will eat its prey whole, rather then pecking off bite-size chunks of flesh.

Tyrannosaurus Rex

Class:	Sauropsida
Order:	Saurischia
Family:	Tyrannosauridae
Genus:	*Tyrannosaurus* (species *T. rex*)
Distribution:	What is now known as western North America, and (possibly) Asia
Habitat:	Semi-tropical, open forest, coastal forested swamp
Diet:	Carnivorous, including (possibly) carrion

Standing at up to 43 feet (13 m) high, Tyrannosuarus rex was one of the largest known land predators, living during the late Cretaceous period (85 to 65 million years ago). Since the first Tyrannosaurus fossil was found in 1902, the animal has become one of the most celebrated of dinosaurs, and more knowledge is gained with every new fossil discovery (of which there have so far been about three thousand). In 1995, paleontologists in Canada found the first T. rex coprolite (fossilized dung), from which much has been revealed about the animal.

MESS FACTOR

5 out of 5

Description

The coprolite discovered in 1995 was found in whitish-green rock, and measured an impressive 17 inches (44 cm) long, 6 inches (15 cm) high, and 5 inches (13 cm) wide. It was found near where a T. rex skeleton was being excavated—a location, along with the coprolite's considerable size, that led scientists to conclude that it was something the animal had left behind. It contained fragments of meat and bone, and, although we can never know for sure, almost certainly did have an unpleasant odor when initially laid.

▲ **This mighty log provides evidence of the T. rex's poor table manners—swallowing food without chewing.**

Primordial Poop

When analyzed, the dung was found to contain shattered chunks of bone located among other, once-soft matter preserved in the form of lithium (turned to rock) phosphate.

The presence of bone chunks in its excrement suggests that T. rex had a short, rapid digestive system, rather than that of a reptile like a snake (see pages 98–9) or crocodile, whose dietary bone components get completely dissolved before excretion. It also provides evidence that T. rex didn't tear off strips of flesh, but instead crushed its food—bones and all—with its teeth before swallowing. Further investigation of the bone fragments, particularly their blood vessels, yielded more information about the prey—in particular, that it was a juvenile herbivorous dinosaur, around the size of a cow.

IN ONE ERA, OUT THE OTHER

A coprolite is one of several trace fossils, the others being fossilized track marks, cololites (fossilized intestines), and regurgitalites (fossilized vomit).

Because dung is so often broken up and decomposed, it is relatively rare to find coprolites. However, other specimens have given clues about dinosaurs and the environments in which they lived. Some have contained burrows, similar to those of dung beetles; others have borne traces of plants, which, when dated, have led to new findings about their evolution. Just as with the contemporary version, fossilized dung provides evidence of the dynamic nature of the environment in which it was laid.

85

Bear

Order: Carnivora

Family: Ursidae

Genera: Various, including American Black (*Ursus americanus*) and Brown (*Ursus arctos*—various subspecies)

Distribution: Wide areas of North America, Europe, Asia

Habitat: Mostly forests or shrubland, semi-open

Diet: Omnivorous, but mostly plants

Measuring up to 10 feet (3 m) on its hind legs, and weighing in at up to 1500 pounds (680 kg), the lumbering bear is one of nature's giants. Its appearance in the wild can trigger excitement and fear, and the same can be said of a steaming pile of bear dung. Does a bear shit in the woods? Hikers certainly do if they catch sight of one unexpectedly.

MESS FACTOR

4 out of 5

Description

Bear scat is usually formed of a number of cylindrical pellets, with a mild aroma when fresh. It will be rich in undigested plant material, such as seeds, grasses, and berries, depending on the type of vegetation consumed. A meatier meal will result in a darker, runnier, stinkier stool. They can measure anything between 1 and 2.75 inches (3 and 7 cm) long.

Leading by the Nose

Bear numbers are becoming critically low in some areas because of habitat destruction, hunting, and trapping. Their dung and the data it contains is proving to be a highly valuable tool in determining remaining numbers and pinpointing areas suitable for reintroduction and relocation. In Washington State, specially trained labrador dogs have been used to sniff it out. Scat analysis is cheaper than, for instance, camera surveillance, and under a microscope much information is yielded about a bear's gender, status, stress levels, and diet. And as the science improves, so the results become increasingly more accurate.

Black or Brown?

It is assumed that, because they are bigger, the brown bear's dung is larger than that of the black. This is not strictly true, and even laboratory tests have proved inconclusive. Knowing the difference between the two species can be useful, particularly if confronted by one. If you find that a bear has indeed shat in the woods, there are signs you can look for to assess the risk it (possibly) represents.

As mentioned opposite, a black, runny stool suggests the presence of a carnivorous bear (thus a potential hiker eater). If the scat is fresh, the grass underneath it will still be green and there'll be no signs of insect colonization. On finding any bear dung out in the wild, you should always be extra vigilant and think seriously about moving on.

SCAT FACT

The contents of black-bear dung has been known to include tin cans, pizza boxes, watches, motorbike chains, and hubcaps.

◀ **If you happen upon a deposit of bear poop, ensure its source is nowhere around before you go in for a closer inspection.**

Polar Bear

Order: Carnivora
Family: Ursidae
Genus: *Ursus* (species *U. maritimus*)
Distribution: Arctic Circle
Habitat: Pack ice and coastal arctic areas
Diet: Carnivorous, including aquatic mammals, fish, sea birds, vegetation, garbage

The polar bear, one of the largest terrestrial mammals, is one of nature's apex predators. Its position at the top of its food chain means that it only ever falls prey to other polar bears (or humans). As the debate rages over the effects of climate change on the bear's icy habitat, its dung, or lack of it, plays an important part in the survival of both it and fellow arctic dwellers.

MESS FACTOR

4 out of 5

Description

The appearance of a polar bear's dung varies with the seasons, as it migrates looking for food. While eating meat (most commonly ringed seal), it will deposit black, odorous scats containing strands of hair. Its diet changes around summer, during which the dung features bits of grass, kelp, bird remnants, and garbage. The color will change as well—to a mix of brown, white, black, and, occasionally, red. The dung appears either as nuggets, logs, or splats.

Mother Love

In late fall, a pregnant polar bear will create its own maternity den—a small space dug into a snow drift on mountainous or hilly slopes near the pack ice. It is here that she will give birth (around November or December), and stay with her cub or cubs for the next few months. Having eaten as much ringed-seal blubber (a favorite meal) as she can during the previous spring, the bear will not eat or drink while in her den. Nor will she urinate or defecate there, keeping the den as clean and disease-free as possible.

Polar bears are highly developed in terms of being able to control their body metabolism, which comes in handy in situations such as when food is scarce or when the females retreat to give birth. Baby cubs are born relatively small, weighing about a four-hundredth of the mother's weight (most other newborn carnivores weigh about one-fiftieth of their parent's mass), which may have something to do with their own waste. A slightly premature bear will be able to excrete its own dung and pee without taxing the mother, whose own body may not have the energy (because she's not eating) to recycle the metabolic waste of the cubs if they were still in the womb.

SCAT FACT

In the winter, when food is scarce, polar-bear dung is eaten by hungry scavengers such as arctic foxes and ivory gulls, forming what is biologically known as a detritus food chain.

▼ **A fibrous bear scat sample, bearing remnants of a grassy meal. Meatier diets make runnier dung.**

Aphid

Class: Insecta
Order: Hemiptera
Family: Ten families
Genera: Various, covering over four thousand different species
Distribution: Worldwide, mainly temperate zones
Habitat: Various, both indoor and outdoor plants
Diet: Herbivorous, mainly plant sap

Known also as greenfly, blackfly, and plant louse, the aphid is a remarkable insect. The female can reproduce without the intervention of a male (via a process called parthenogenesis), the young can develop to adult status within a few days, and the species are able to reproduce at a phenomenal rate, leading to frequent plant infestations. This, together with the fact that their anal secretions damage the plant host, wins the aphid no friends among gardeners and farmers. Ants, however, love them.

MESS FACTOR

1 out of 5

Description

The appearance of aphid excretion on the leaves of a plant can make many agriculturalists and horticulturalists despair. Initially showing as a glossy shine, it soon turns to a black, sooty mold on the leaf surface, caused by a fungus that soon starts to attack the plant.

Sweet Like Chocolate?

In fact, aphid poo is not much of a poo at all; it is sweet, sticky, and even has its own fragrant-sounding name, "honeydew." It is formed primarily from plant sap—the liquid that contains the nutrients necessary for a plant's survival.

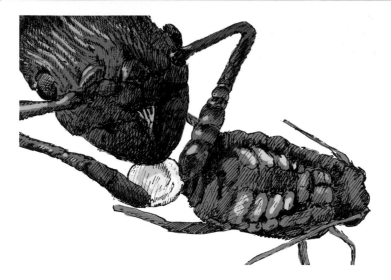

▲ **An aphid squeezing out a drop of honeydew for an appreciative ant. Poop is not always brown and stinky.**

The aphid taps into sap-transportation channels with its long, needle-like mouthpart. It only needs to take a portion of the original nutrients for itself, and adds its own enzymes to the mix before excretion.

Aphids and their sticky poo can be controlled using insecticides, but these often prove harmful to other organisms. More sensible is to employ some of the aphid's natural predators such as ladybugs, parasitic wasps, and so on. Ants would NOT make a suitable choice, though, as they are junkies for the stuff, and indeed may see off a predator rather than see their supply interrupted. An ant will stroke a feeding aphid with its antennae, and is soon presented with a sugary droplet secreted by the aphid from its anus. The amino acids, minerals, and vitamins present in the honeydew-drop are valued so highly by the ant that it will in turn protect the aphid. One ant species, *Lasius neoniger*, will even store and care for the eggs of root aphids, *Geoica* spp., over winter. When the eggs hatch in early spring, the ants will transport them to grass to feed.

POO ON TOAST

Ants are not the only aphid farmers. Bees also love honeydew, and the resulting honey, which is dark and strong, is regarded as "the shit" by connoisseurs.

Bat

Order: Chiroptera

Family: Various

Genera: Various, including Common Pipistrelle (*Pipistrellus pipistrellus*) and Common Vampire (*Desmodus rotundus*)

Distribution: Worldwide, except Arctic and Antarctic

Habitat: Caves, rock crevices, trees, some manmade structures

Diet: Omnivorous, including fruit, nectar, insects

Many myths surround the nocturnal bat, the only mammal to have evolved with true powered flight: that it is blind, that it sucks blood, that it gets in your hair, that it inspired a man called Bruce Wayne to start wearing his underpants over his tights and go out fighting crime in Gotham City. The reality of its poop, or guano, is just as rich: It can sustain a whole ecosystem, can knock a man dead, and can keep roses very happy indeed.

MESS FACTOR

4 out of 5

Description

As with many animals, the dung reflects the food. If the bat has been eating insects, its guano will consist of a series of small, dry, cylindrical pellets, not unlike mouse droppings. If it has been munching on fruit, expect a more wet and formless splodge. Bat guano is high in nutrients such as nitrogen, potassium, and phosphorous, and in more densely populated colonies it is harvested for sale as garden fertilizer.

To the Bat Cave!

Bat guano can be highly toxic, particularly when it is sitting in a cave without much fresh air, under a colony of a million bats providing a never-ending fresh supply. The droppings are so high in ammonia that they can easily burn nasal passages. Diseases associated with bat guano include rabies, SARS, and other viral and fungal infections. Histoplasmosis is a disease transmitted via guano, although if contracted via the bats living near the pyramids of Egypt, it is known by the more romantic name, "Curse of the Mummy's Tomb." This is of little comfort, however, to any unfortunate person who suffers a respiratory shutdown thanks to a bit of bat poo.

Bat guano, however, is not a solely malicious force; it provides far more than it takes away. The floors of those caves, feet deep in spongy excreta, are not inert symbols of decay, but are instead home to a wide range of fauna—snakes, toads, geckos, beetles—that thrive in these conditions. The dung that is good for the garden is just as good, if not better, for these self-contained mini-ecosystems situated right at the source. All the nutrients any self-respecting guanovore (poop-eating creature) could wish for are here. And what fills up the guanovore will also fill up its predator. And what fills up the predator, will also fill up the predator's predator. And so on, right up the food chain.

SCAT FACT

Thanks to its high phosphorus and nitrogen count, bat guano was used to make gunpowder during the Civil War.

▼ **Resembling a fat load of burnt mince, accumulations of bat poop create and sustain whole ecosystems.**

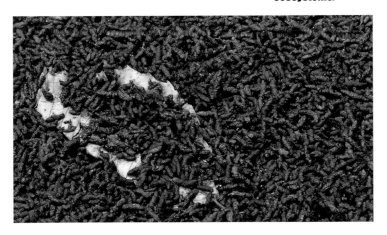

Plankton

Classification: Plankton is a collective term for a wide variety of organisms, both plant and animal

Distribution: Worldwide

Habitat: Oceans, seas, and lakes

Diet: Various nutrients, including nitrate, phosphate, light, minerals, sinking material from surface water

One single scoop from the abyssal plain at the very bottom of the ocean, some 2.5 miles (4 km) down, recently revealed nearly 400 new species of worms, crustaceans, and other previously undiscovered organisms. Although still in its infancy, research into plankton and its poop has already revealed much about what lies beneath, as well as its potential for life above, the surface.

MESS FACTOR

1 out of 5

Description

Of the three main types of plankton, it is only zooplankton that actually produces feces. These are animals that feed on other plankton, and include tiny crustaceans (like krill), the larvae or immature stages of larger animals, and single-celled animals. The poop is ejected near the water surface, from where it drifts with the tidal current.

Excrement Environment

Gathering any plankton for analysis is a challenge. The word *plankton* is derived from the Greek meaning "wanderer" or "drifter," because they are organisms that cannot swim or float in any direction other than with the oceanic current. Most of their movement is horizontal, so the best harvesting devices are those that are untethered and follow their quarry through the water. Recent developments include the precision-based Twilight Zone Explorer (TZEX), which sweeps along with the currents, collecting samples as it goes.

The material through which the TZEX floats is a complex mixture of zooplankton feces, dead zooplankton, and dead phytoplankton. This mix is called "marine snow," and it plays an important part in transporting nutrients down to deeper sea levels. The zooplankton poop is additionally important because, providing it eventually sinks, it will transport away from the water's surface the excess carbon produced by phytoplankton as they photosynthesize. The feces of zooplankton such as krill or salp are relatively heavy and ideal for the job; lighter, crumblier poo will leave the carbon unabsorbed. This has ramifications for the environment at large, as the world struggles to keep its carbon emissions to a minimum. By preventing the seaborne carbon from re-entering the atmosphere, heavy plankton poop is doing its bit for the planet.

SCAT FACT

Measuring as little as 0.000007874 inches (200 nanometers), plankton poop is the smallest in the world.

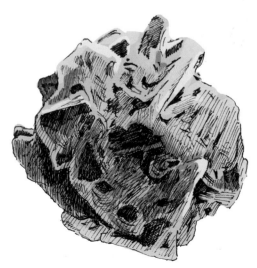

▶ **A microscopic view of zooplankton poop. Providing it sinks instead of floating, such feces aids in minimizing carbon levels in the atmosphere.**

Snail

Phylum: Mollusca

Class: Gastropoda

Orders: Various families and genera, covering a total of over eighty thousand species

Distribution: Worldwide

Habitat: Various, including freshwater, marine, terrestrial

Diet: Herbivorous (though there are exceptions), including leaves, fruit, lichen

Snails can prove to be either perfect pets or problematic pests. On farmland they can damage crops, whereas in fish tanks and aquariums they will feed on fish excreta and algae, doing their bit to keep the water clean. The familiar thick slime of mucus is not the only moist secretion that a snail can leave behind, however ...

MESS FACTOR

2 out of 5

Description

Diet plays its part in the appearance of a snail's shell (affecting coloration as the snail grows) and of its feces, which emerges from under the shell looking like a tiny piece of folded rope. It is moist when fresh, and dries to a more brittle texture over time. The poop also smells pretty badly if the snail has been feeding on wet food.

Where Does It Come From?

So how does a snail poo? Most of the organs are found in the visceral hump, which is covered by the shell. A piece of food is broken off and ground down by the radula in the snail's mouth. The radula is a membrane that contains the nearest a snail has to teeth. Made of chitin (a hard substance that is also a main component of shells and insect

96

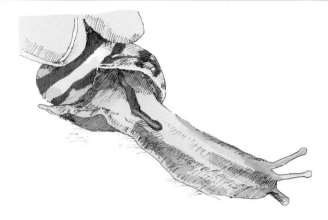

exoskeletons), these "teeth" break down the food by drawing it over a ridge of cartilage. The food is broken down further by digestive juices as it then passes through the esophagus, the stomach, and the intestine. Whatever waste is left is then ready to be excreted from the snail's anal pore, which is situated near the shell's rim, at the head end. So the food does its own spiral journey, around the organs and back out near where it came in.

Agriculture

In 2003, one species of American marine snail, *Littoraria irrorata*, was discovered using its poo in a unique form of fungal agriculture. The snail works its way through marsh grass, creating the telltale holes and defecating as it goes. Contained in the poop are fungal spores that then flourish—not only do the spores have access to the leaf's inner tissue (thanks to the snail's mouth), they have also been deposited in a nutrient-rich fertilizer (thanks to its butt). The snail then returns to the spot where a fresh crop of its favorite fungal growth is waiting for it. Such farming had been observed in insects before (see Termites, pages 100–101), but never before among mollusks.

▲ **The snail's food spirals around the inner shell and is dunged at the front in a typically rope-like form.**

ONCE LICKED . . .

You can catch meningitis from a snail—but only by licking it.

Snake

Class:	Sauropsida
Order:	Squamata
Families:	Various, including several genera and around 2,700 species
Distribution:	Worldwide, except Ireland, Iceland, Hawaii, New Zealand, most of Antarctica
Habitat:	Various, including desert, urban, forest
Diet:	Carnivorous, including rodents, small reptiles, birds, other snakes

With the smallest worm snake measuring around 6 inches (15 cm) long, and the biggest green anaconda taking up nearly 30 feet (9 m) and weighing up to 550 pounds (250 kg), snakes do indeed come in all shapes and sizes. Well, all sizes at least. The sight of one can inspire fear and terror in some people, while others keep them as pets. Whatever the species, their dunging habits are really quite inoffensive (apart from the smell).

MESS FACTOR

4 out of 5

Description

The size of the dropping depends on the size of the species, but all snakes leave a cord-like deposit with constrictions and undulations along it. Normally light or dark brown, with a tip of white uric acid at one end, the poop dries to a chalky residue. Indigestible matter such as fur and claws may sometimes be visible. The smell is strong, and some snakes can go for weeks without dunging.

Open Wide

A snake will kill its prey either by biting it, crushing it, or eating it alive, and all prey is swallowed whole. The snake doesn't chew, but the flexibility of its lower jaw allows the food to

▲ **Feces and uric acid fresh from the rear of a small domestic snake. The animal dungs infrequently, but the strong smell sure lets you know when it has.**

pass into the digestive system relatively intact. When it is not eating, the snake is storing up the energy necessary for successful digestion, as it is an intensive process. Strong acidic enzymes and gastric juices in the stomach and intestine break down proteins and absorb nutrients, and what is left (mostly insoluble matter like hair and bone) will pass into the animal's cloaca, from where it is excreted. This whole process can take weeks.

Home Cooking

Keeping a pet snake is not like having a cat; it requires specialist knowledge and equipment. For a start, snakes can get some serious illnesses from their poop. Unlike in the wild, a snake in an unclean tank is forced to hang out with its own dung—and nobody wants to do that. Such a situation will weaken the snake and make it less able to fight infections. Snakes also like a warm ambient temperature, and if too cold they will try to hog any available heat source. This can result in the contents of their intestines getting cooked by any directional heat source, which, unsurprisingly, causes a lot of discomfort and can cause fecaliths, or fecal stones. Although snakes may look tough, they need TLC just as much as we all do.

POO OFF

Although not strictly poop, the garter snake emits a noxious secretion from its anal gland when picked up or threatened. Not so much a case of shitting itself, more a case of "Leave me alone!"

Termite

Order:	Isoptera
Class:	Insecta
Distribution:	Within 50 degrees north and south of the equator
Habitat:	Various, including tropical rainforest, desert, shrubland
Diet:	Cellulose, dead plant material, other detritus

Termites live in highly organized, densely populated colonies that can total several million individuals. Much smaller numbers can cause significant damage to buildings and crops, and the appearance of their poop, called "frass," is a telltale sign of an infestation. Frass plays an important part in various areas of termite life, including nest construction, nutrition, and health.

MESS FACTOR

1 out of 5

Description

Termites can be grouped depending on what they feed on, and the appearance of their frass will alter accordingly. Drywood termite frass, for example, is formed of a number of tiny, almost hexagonal pellets, which are hard and dry (three pairs of anal glands extract water from the waste just before excretion). Subterranean termite frass, however, is muddy. Different species deposit their frass in different places, too, and the color will reflect whatever they have been eating.

Ass Fulla Frass

All termite colonies consist of various castes—workers, soldiers, alates (reproductive termites), and a queen—but it is the workers who get to

Frass is not the only anal secretion common to termites. The queen squeezes out juice as a "thank you" to the workers who lift her around when she is pregnant (at which time she grows up to 100 times her original size), and digested food is also distributed around the colony via workers' butts.

▼ **Frass plays various roles within termite colonies, and its presence in buildings is a sign of infestation.**

handle the most frass. It is mixed with soil, chewed wood, and saliva, and used to make their highly elaborate nests and tunnel systems, resulting in a construction material so hard that, in some savannah areas, people have used it for their own buildings. In more urban areas, the frass is similarly mixed with soil and plant matter to create tubes through which the colony can pass over any indigestible material to get from the earth to the rotting wood. These typically appear on brickwork on the outside of a building.

Like snails, termites have developed a talent for farming their own crop of fungus. Within the nest, fungus "gardens" are cultivated with frass as fertilizer. Once eaten, the fungal spores pass through the termites undigested, so being able to germinate freely in a fresh frass batch. Frass is also of potential antibiotic benefit to the colony. Dead termites are always buried in separate chambers and covered in the stuff, leading some to suggest that it has antibacterial properties and this is one way to keep any infection from spreading.

Turtle

Class: Sauropsida
Order: Testudines
Family: Various
Genera: Various, including Leatherback (*Dermochelys coriacea*)
Distribution: Worldwide, except Antarctica
Habitat: Various, including ocean, river, marshland
Diet: Omnivorous, including insects, crustaceans, jellyfish, algae, fruit

Turtles are an ancient group of animals that have been represented in fossils dating back 20 million years. They have outlived dinosaurs and several ice ages, and as individuals can live as long as 175 years—heroes in a half-shell indeed. The animals can be confused with their relatives, the tortoise and the terrapin. For the sake of argument, they're all welcome here.

MESS FACTOR

3 out of 5

Description

The state of a turtle's turd depends on the size of its creator, and what it ate. However, most turtle dung is compact, moist when fresh, and can resemble human feces. Unlike humans', though, turtle poop doesn't pose a big health risk, flies don't like it, and it's relatively odor-free.

Mutant Ninja Turtle Poop

In 1989, health officials on the island of Oahu in northern Hawaii were mystified by the appearance of a floating mass of poop coming in from the sea and washing up on one of the region's most scenic and popular beaches. It was initially blamed on turtles resident just off the Hawaiian coast. Matters turned more serious, however, when similar flotillas came ashore accompanied by a lot of human garbage like cigarette butts and plastic, suggesting that the turtles were innocent, and either day-trippers, cruise-ship passengers, or leaky pipes weren't. The mystery was eventually resolved, over ten years later, when a faulty sewage system was finally identified and repaired.

WonderPoo

The green sea turtle (*Chelonia mydas*) lives in tropical and subtropical waters around the world, and it's possible that, like the koala bear, eating parental poop plays an important part in its development, and that of its environment. Specialized microorganisms that help the adult turtle digest cellulose from the algae it feeds on may be passed to the juvenile through scatophagy (poop-eating). This is only a theory, however, and one rejected by some biologists. Other animals, like the hermit crab (*Coenobita rugosus*) have also been observed tucking into a turtle pile, while the dung itself has been suggested as a possible means of effective seed dispersal, particularly among those living in forest areas, such as the box turtles.

LOG JAM

Turtles kept as pets should be properly cared for. Water supplies should be changed often to prevent an unwanted build-up of poop, which can otherwise lead to infection and poor health.

▼ **An example of poop from an African spurred tortoise kept in captivity. The grassy remains point to its plant-based diet.**

Whale

Order: Cetacea

Family: Various; nine families, including Balaenopteridae and Megapterinae

Genera: Various; species include Sperm (*Physeter macrocephalus*) and Humpback (*Megaptera novaeangliae*)

Distribution: Worldwide

Habitat: Ocean

Diet: Carnivorous, including krill, fish, mammals

One of nature's Goliaths, the whale is celebrated the world over for its size, its power, and the ability of its mating call to ease childbirth. Measuring up to 110 feet (33 m) long and weighing up to 110 tons (181,000 kg), the blue whale is the largest animal on Earth. Fittingly, its dung is the biggest, too, although this is difficult to assess properly because of its consistency. While some species are endangered, whales are still subject to hunting, making them politically controversial. What may just save the whale, though, is its poo.

MESS FACTOR

3 out of 5

Description

Whale poo has a high water content, and so tends to dissipate into a large cloud as it reaches the water, instead of sinking as a humungous log. It sits dispersed on the water surface like a large stain, then slowly sinks to the sea bed, providing nutrition for life below. Its color will alter with changes in its diet (a mouthful of shrimp, for instance, will result in a pink cloud). Because of the tremendous pressure under water, whales dung near the surface, and contained within will be undigested fish eyes, squid beaks, and so on, as well as soft fecal matter.

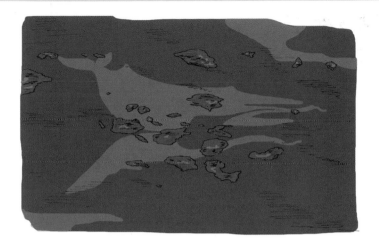

▲ **Different-colored poop reflects changes in the whale's diet, such as this pink shrimp-based emission.**

WHAT PUKED THAT?

Ambergris, known as "floating gold" because of the high price it attracts, is often confused with whale poop. It is actually indigestible bone fragments vomited from the sperm whale's mouth (similar, in theory at least, to owl pellets), and eventually dries to form a sweet-smelling musk.

Whale Digestion, A to Z

There are two kinds of whale, differentiated by the way they take in food. Baleen whales have sieve-like baleens which filter food through the mouth, while toothed whales have teeth that help them to seize and tear. Neither suborder chews their food, but both have four-chambered stomachs, the first chamber of which contains sand and broken shells which crush the food into smaller, more manageable pieces, similar to the function of stones in an owl's gizzard (see pages 82–83). A huge pair of kidneys regulates the freshwater levels in their bodies by dealing with the high salt content of their diet. Although the whale has a cloaca, it urinates and defecates separately.

Safe from Harm?

One of the justifications used for continued whaling is that it serves a scientific purpose, as in slicing one open to find out more about it. Thanks to DNA technology, anti-whalers believe that that argument won't hold water for much longer. Australian researchers have found that fresh poop samples, freshly sieved from the sea, can reveal as much information about the animal and in a wholly non-invasive way.

Civet

Order: Carnivora

Family: Viverridae

Genera: Various, including Giant (*Macrogalidia musschenbroekii*) and Otter (*Cynogale bennettii*)

Distribution: Parts of Africa, Asia, and Europe

Habitat: Prefers tropical rainforest, also woodland and savannah

Diet: Omnivorous, including small mammals, birds, fruit, eggs, crustaceans

Although often referred to as the "civet cat," this animal has no feline lineage. With its long tail and pointed face, the civet came to be regarded as something of a pest in its native lands, and was often hunted for its meat. Over recent years, the civet's dung has had a colorful history, being both condemned as lethal and heralded as a sign of luxury. Ever had a coffee that tasted like shit? This animal may well have had something to do with it...

MESS FACTOR

4 out of 5

Description

Civet scat is roughly textured, containing much semi-digested and even entirely undigested material, the latter including coffee beans (see below). It is generally deposited in middens known as "civetries." Civets being elusive, nocturnal creatures, civetries are often one of the few signs of their presence in an area.

Deadly Dung

In 2002 and 2003, an outbreak of a new strain of Severe Acute Respiratory Syndrome (SARS) caused the deaths of nearly eight hundred people, mostly in China. The civet was identified as a vector species (host) for the virus after tests were

POO-FUME

Another anal secretion used for luxury products is the musk from the civet's perineal glands, which employed as a stabilizing agent in perfumes. Demand has led to the illegal farming of the animal, with the glands forcibly scraped every few days for maximum musk return. Top fashion houses are being urged to switch to more synthetic substitutes.

conducted on meat from markets in Guangdong Province, where the first cases were recorded. Contact with the animal's dung was seen as highly dangerous, and health officials ordered a mass cull of some ten thousand animals in early 2004.

Wake Up and Smell the Civet Shit

While Chinese civets were getting it in the neck, the Indonesian palm civet (*Paradoxurus hermaphroditus*) was enjoying some red-carpet treatment. For years the animal annoyed local coffee farmers, skulking around the plantations, stealing the ripest fruits that contained the best beans. These beans passed straight through, undigested, and out the other end. Someone, somewhere, hit upon the idea of actually reusing the beans from the dung, roasting them as usual. The resulting blend, called "kopi luwak," is now the world's rarest and most expensive coffee (one cup will set you back about $50). It is believed that enzymes particular to the palm civet's stomach release some of the bean's proteins during digestion, removing much of the bitterness in favor of a gentler aroma and taste.

▼ **Undigested coffee beans found in a wet civet splat are used to make the world's most expensive cup of joe.**

Wombat

Order: Diprotodontia
Family: Vombatidae
Genera: Various; species include Common (*Vombatus ursinus*)
Distribution: Mostly southern Australia
Habitat: Various, including open forest, scrubland, plain
Diet: Herbivorous, including grasses, bark, roots

The solitary, nocturnal wombat is a usually timid creature, though aggressive if provoked. It would rather go through an object than around it, and so has been known to damage walls and doors. Physically similar to a small bear, the wombat spends most of its time underground in its burrow. It also deposits one of the most characteristic, beautifully formed poos in the world.

MESS FACTOR

2 out of 5

Description

Composed of four to eight separate cube-shaped pellets, each roughly 0.75 inches (2 cm) wide, wombat dung is dark brown or black, and greener inside. The texture is fine but fibrous, and it smells much like the animal itself (a sweet, peaty odor). The pellets are left as territorial markers in areas such as rubbing posts, and their shape means they stay where they're deposited for longer. The animal also scores the ground with its front paws while dunging, leaving a clear V-shaped mark.

Food-Focused

The digestive system of a wombat is highly efficient. Their teeth are continually growing, meaning they are always kept sharp for chewing.

Their low metabolism (one meal can take up to two weeks to digest fully) enables them to extract maximum nutrition from their relatively poor diet, which is high in fiber and low in protein. Once out the other end, the resulting dung is some of the driest recorded.

Natural Ordure

Wombat dung has led to the scientific discovery of twenty-four new species of fly. Two species of the Borboroidini fly, native to Australia, were found to be attracted to the dung and proved more prevalent in areas with high wombat populations. This encouraged entomologists to focus on the dung alone, resulting in a huge growth in known species. A symbiosis of flora and fauna exclusive to one geographical area, represented by this relationship, is important when considering issues like species protection and management.

The northern hairy-nosed wombat (*Lasiorhinus krefftii*) is a critically endangered animal, with just one single colony occupying a 1.8 mile (3 km) square patch of forest in central Queensland. Its dung is playing a different role in its conservation, with biologists extracting hormones contained in the poop to monitor reproductive status and determine population breeding rates.

BUTT OUT

The wombat's rear is formed of a very tough hide made of cartilage. Under attack from a predator in the burrow, the wombat will use its rump as a shield.

▶ **Saving the best until last—the fine, dry, geometric dung of the wombat must surely rank as one of nature's most beautiful specimens.**

Index

Credits

Image Credits:

Photographs on pages 23, 39, and 53 © ZSL
Other photographs courtesy of Shutterstock, iStockPhoto, and Matt Pagett
All illustrations by Matt Pagett

Matt would like to thank:

Colchester Zoo, U.K. (www.colchester-zoo.co.uk)
Repco, Brighton, U.K. (www.repcoreptiles.co.uk)
Marwell Zoological Park, U.K. (www.marwell.org.uk)
Linda J. Gormezano, American Museum of Natural History, New York, U.S.A.
Tim Myles, University of Toronto, Canada
Benny Thomas, for original inspiration
Prince, the cat with the stinkiest scat
Mike at rehabdesign and all at Quid

Dedicated to the memory of my nan.